LISTEN!
MUSIC AND CIVILIZATION

pcy font ceulx z celles . qui ont
fait le pfaultier.

Listen!
Music and civilization

GEOFFREY BRACE

AND

IAN BURTON

CAMBRIDGE UNIVERSITY PRESS
Cambridge
London · Melbourne

by the same authors LISTEN! MUSIC AND NATURE
LISTEN! MUSIC AND YOU

Published by the Syndics of the Cambridge University Press
The Pitt Building, Trumpington Street, Cambridge CB2 IRP
Bentley House, 200 Euston Road, London NWI 2DB
296 Beaconsfield Parade, Middle Park, Melbourne 3206, Australia

© Cambridge University Press 1978

ISBN 0 521 21153 0

First published 1978

Book designed by Peter Ducker

Printed in Great Britain by
Ebenezer Baylis & Son Ltd, Leicester and London

Thanks are due to the following for permission to reproduce
extracts:
Hänssler-Verlag for 'Le Ballet Comique de la Royne', published
through the American Institute of Musicology in the series
Musicological Studies & Documents, translated and transcribed by
Carol and Lander MacClintock. © 1971 by Armen Carapetyan;
American Institute of Musicology/Hänssler-Verlag, Neuhausen-
Stuttgart, W. Germany. Used by permission.
George Allen & Unwin Ltd for 'Blind Men' from *The Book of Songs*
by Arthur Waley.
Oxford University Press for an extract from *Naples and Neopolitan
Opera* by Michael F. Robinson.

Thanks are due to the following for permission to reproduce words
and music:
Dover Publications for 'Bound for the Promised Land' from
Spiritual Folk Songs of Early America by G. Pullen Jackson.
Ascherberg, Hopwood and Crew Ltd for 'The Boy I Love is up in the
Gallery' by George Ware.
'Haralambis' from *Folk Songs of Greece* arranged and translated by
Susan and Ted Alevizos © 1968 Oak Publications, a division of
Embassy Music Corporation, New York. All rights reserved. Used
by permission.
'The Final Song from the Festivities for the Marriage of Cosimo I of
Florence' reprinted from *A Renaissance Entertainment* by Andrew C.
Minor & M. Bonner Mitchell by permission of the University of
Missouri Press, copyright 1968 by the Curators of the University of
Missouri.
J. M. Dent & Sons Ltd for 'Venite a laudare per amore' from *Music in
the Middle Ages* by G. Reese.
The Essex Music Group for 'Union Maid' and 'No more My Lord'.

Contents

Thanks are due to the following for permission to reproduce photographs and other illustrations: Barnaby's Picture Library, cover, p. 45; The Mansell Collection, frontispiece, pp. 15, 18(b, e), 22(b), 27, 43(a, c), 55(a), 56(c), 62(a), 69(c); Radio Times Hulton Picture Library, pp. 1, 2, 18(g), 41, 43(b), 48(a, b), 49, 50(b), 51(a), 52(b, d, e, f), 55(b), 56(a, b), 57, 58(a), 59(a, b, c, d), 60, 62(b, c); Camera Press, pp. 5, 17(b), 58(b), 73(a, b, e, f); British Museum, p. 7(a); Society for Anglo-Chinese Understanding, p. 7(b); Keystone Press Agency Ltd, pp. 10, 14, 32, 35(a), 37, 73(d); Japan Information Centre, p. 11(a, b, c); Douglas Dickens, pp. 13, 36; Navosti Press Agency, p. 17(a); The Embassy of the Hungarian Peoples Republic, p. 18(a); Elisabeth Speidel, p. 18(c); Derek Allen and EMI Ltd, p. 18(d); EMI Ltd, pp. 18(f), 71(e); The Dean & Chapter of Worcester Cathedral, p. 21; Bildarchiv Preussischer Kulturbesitz, p. 22(a); Anne Bolt, p. 25; York Festival, p. 26(a); Salzburg Festival, p. 26(b); Swiss National Tourist Office, p. 34; Victoria and Albert Museum, p. 35(b); National Coal Board, p. 46; Abbas Hashemi, p. 50(a); BBC, p. 51(b); Savoy Hotel, p. 52(a, c); Roger Viollet, p. 53; Houston Rogers, p. 54; Mary Evans Picture Library, p. 61; Radio City Music Hall, p. 64; Culver Pictures Inc., pp. 65, 72; CBS, pp. 67(a, c), 69(a); RCA Records, p. 67(b); Rogers & Cowan Inc., p. 67(d); MGM Records, p. 67(e); Springer/ Bettmann Archive, p. 68(a); Melody Maker, p. 68(b); AM Records, p. 68(c); Evolution, p. 69(b); Atlantic Records, p. 71(a); Pye Records, pp. 71(b), 73(c); The Decca Record Company Ltd, p. 71(c); Anchor, p. 71(d).
The drawings are by Ted Draper.

Music and civilization

This book is about music as it is used in civilized societies—what people use it for, how it comes about, and the types of music people ask for and enjoy in different circumstances and in different times and places.

We have tried not to duplicate the kind of information which appears in the normal music history, but hope that this book will provide a framework into which the inquiring student can fit his subsequent musical experience.

1 · The East

The word 'civilization' means the life of people who have established permanent communities. So we start with the music of the first cities. These were in Mesopotamia and the people were called Sumerians.

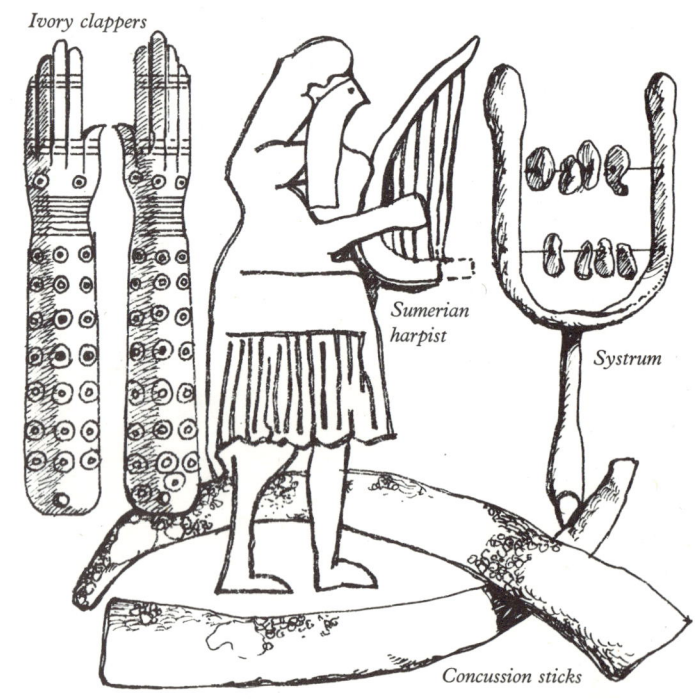

An Assyrian king and his queen feasting to music.

The Sumerians had a king, officials, an army, laws, streets, shops, gardens, palaces. They also had sculpture, painting, poetry and music.

Music was for three things:

> temple services
> court entertainment
> peasant labour and recreation.

Temple music was highly organized. There were hymns and prayers for each season, each day, each god, each kind of ceremony. Funerals, weddings, coronations, etc., all had their special music.

Court music was in the hands of the king's harpists, singers and dancers such as you see on the old friezes. For many centuries after they happened, kings liked to hear epic songs about past glories and great conquests, and legends about their gods and about how the world began.

Peasant music has probably changed little in the last four thousand years. In fact, if we want to know just what the music of those carved figures sounded like or how David sang to Saul, we need only listen to a present-day Egyptian boatman or Jordanian farmer to get a very good idea.

Ivory clappers

Sumerian harpist

Systrum

Concussion sticks

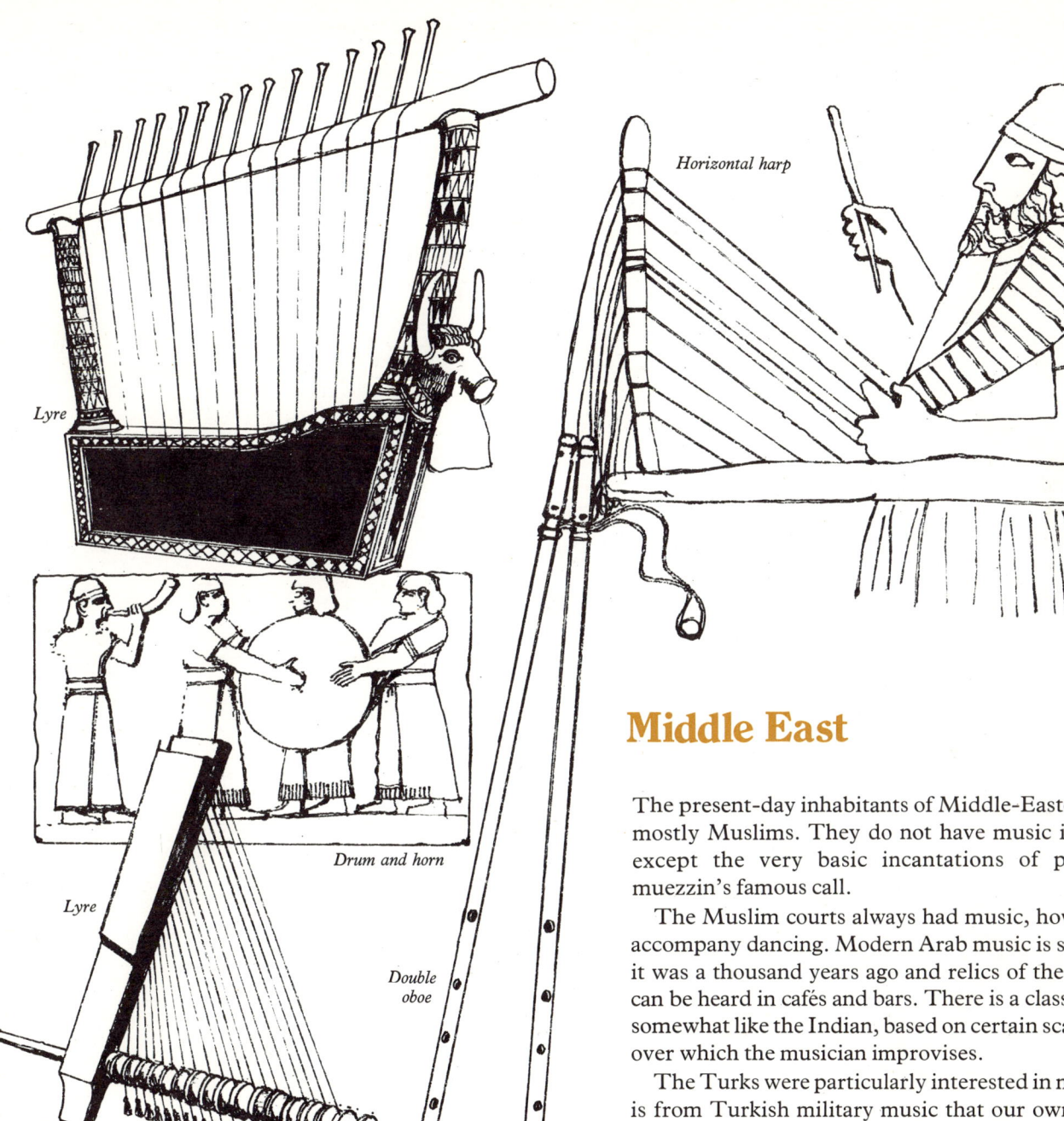

Horizontal harp

Lyre

Lyre

Drum and horn

Double oboe

Middle East

The present-day inhabitants of Middle-Eastern countries are mostly Muslims. They do not have music in their mosques except the very basic incantations of prayers and the muezzin's famous call.

The Muslim courts always had music, however, mainly to accompany dancing. Modern Arab music is still very much as it was a thousand years ago and relics of the old court music can be heard in cafés and bars. There is a classical Arab music, somewhat like the Indian, based on certain scales and rhythms over which the musician improvises.

The Turks were particularly interested in military music. It is from Turkish military music that our own military bands evolved, by way of the crusaders. It was the Turks who had drums on horses, cymbals and drums to strike fear into the

3

enemy and shrill reedpipes which we called shawms and later oboes. Viennese musicians like Haydn and Mozart in the eighteenth century often heard Turkish music and imitated it in their own pieces–Haydn's 'Military' Symphony and Mozart's 'Rondo alla Turca.'

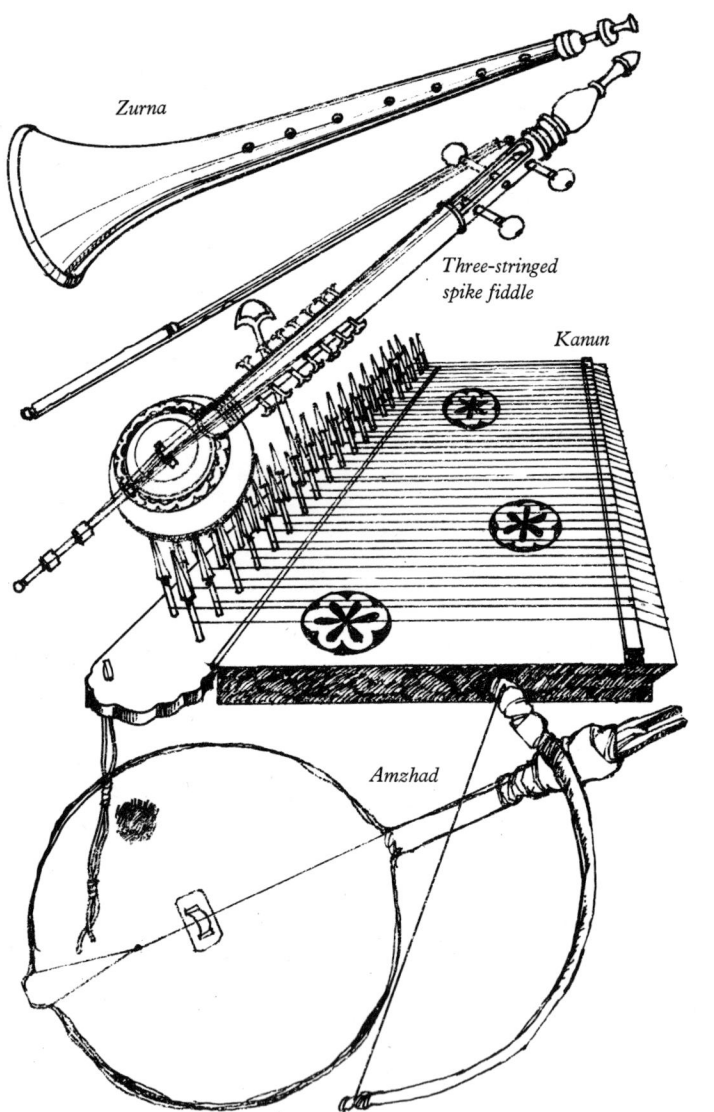

Zurna

Three-stringed spike fiddle

Kanun

Amzhad

Jewish chant for Psalm 144

Le - do - vid bo - ruh a - do - noi___ tsu - ri___

ham - la - med___ jo - dai la - krov ets -

- be - o ssaj la - mil___ ho - mo___

Folksong from Iraq, for recorder, flute, oboe or violin

Accompany with drone G and F

4

Instruments (from left) : front row—vichitra veena, sarod, sitar, sarod; back row—sarangi, sarswati veena, mirdang.

India

Indian music has become well known in the West in recent times. We must remember that there is Indian 'classical' music and Indian 'folk' music. The folk music is simple melody and rhythmic accompaniment. Many of the songs and dances have simple tunes like those of other countries; some have rather more complicated rhythms as this is a feature of Indian music generally. The classical music is what we hear mostly in Europe. It is based on some very complicated theories to be found in old instruction books dating back to the sixth century and takes a lifetime to master. It is an improvised music—like jazz—and the performance is the thing; the musician does not play a piece—there is no such thing as

a 'piece' in Indian classical music. He plays an improvisation based on a certain scale pattern called a 'rag' of which there are about sixty in normal use.

The player varies the pattern in many ways—he invents tunes based on it, he plays with rhythms, he ornaments notes with slides and trills, he flattens notes or sharpens them (sometimes a lot, sometimes just a little), he makes notes 'wobble' by pulling at the strings (which are much looser on Indian instruments). The accompanying drummer (the drums are called 'tabla') also makes a very personal variation of certain accepted rhythmic patterns and combines with the player of the melody instrument.

A song to teach the rag 'Bhupkalian'

Sa - dhe su-ra sa - dhe_ Sa-dhe su-ra sa - dhe_

su-ra su-ra-lo - ka de - na Sa-dhe su-ra sa - dhe_

au - da-va ye-hi ra - ga sam-gi-ta ma-ta pra-ma-na

SA RE GA PA DHA SA DHA PA GA RE

SA u-ta-la-po-la-ta su-ra-na-ki___

sa-dhe su-ra sa - dhe_ sa-dhe. A pentatonic scale with
E as its centre

SOME TYPICAL INDIAN TABLA RHYTHMS

Indian rhythms are based on a pattern of accented beats – what we would call a pattern of different bar-lengths. For example:

this pattern is then repeated and used as the basis for many rhythmic variations.

SOME OTHER RAGS

Bibhas

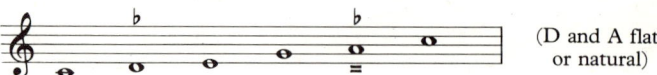

(D and A flat or natural)

Bahar

Bhairavi

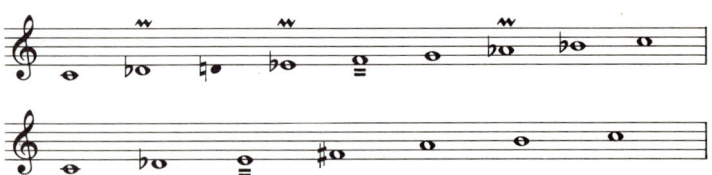

= is the central note.

∼ turn on these notes.

• only used as a stepping note between two others.

Try your own improvisation on these rags.

(All notes can be decorated with slides and microtonal ornaments.)

China

Chinese music also has very complicated theories attached to it, especially legends about how music began and how the various notes of the scale were arrived at. But, in fact, Chinese music is one of the most straightforward of Eastern styles. Rhythms are often in clear twos and fours with simple division of the main notes (crotchets) into half beats (quavers) and rarely smaller. The melodies are based on the five-note–pentatonic–scale CDEGA with occasional decorating semitones, like the classical 'appoggiatura' which they call 'pien tones'.

There is no harmony as we know it. Some instruments will play a drone or two–or even a sustained full chord (the 'sheng' can do this). Melody instruments playing together will play in 'heterophony'–each person playing his own variation of the tune at the same time; a style of group playing found all over the East.

The singing is generally high pitched and nasal, rather strident to our ears and, again, never in harmony.

In modern China, music has an important social role to play and many of the old traditions are maintained. There is a strong Western influence. All European orchestral instruments are used and European styles of composing are copied with Chinese 'accents'. One of the most popular instruments is the accordion which the Chinese took from the Soviet Union but adapted to their own pentatonic tuning.

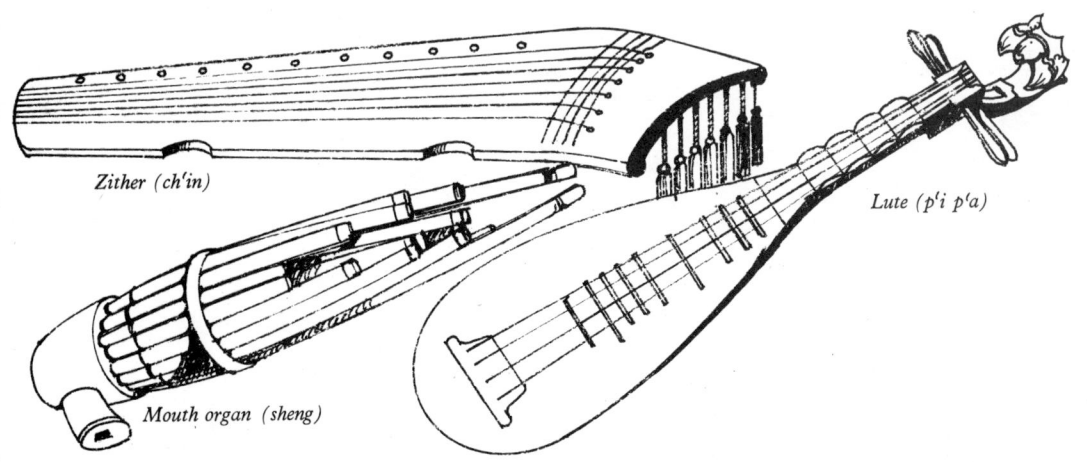

Zither (ch'in)

Mouth organ (sheng)

Lute (p'i p'a)

Chinese wedding march

The stone chime (pien-ch'ing) is comprised of 16 stones suspended on a frame. The stones are of equal length and breadth, differing only in thickness: the thicker the stone the deeper the sound.

OLD RITUAL MUSIC

The ceremonies for the worship of Confucius had very precise musical instructions.

'When the Emperor enters the temple the Guiding Music ceases and the most profound silence reigns. Everybody is at his place; the singers, the harpers, the sheng players and small drums are ranged on the west and east sides within the temple; the bell and stone instruments, the flutes and larger drums are outside. On the marble terrace are thirty-six dancers divided into two groups, one west and one east.

When the Emperor arrives before the shrine, the Grand Master of Ceremonies gives the signal to commence by beating the little drum he holds in his hand. At this signal the flags are raised, the leader beats his instrument three times and the whole band begins to play.

- The bell sounds the note of the verse.

- The bell chime gives one sound at each word.

- After the bell chime, the lutes give their note, followed by all the other instruments except the stone chime which is struck after all the other instruments in order to "receive the sound and transmit it to the second note".

- At the end of the verse a drum is beaten three times and answered by another.

- The bell chime then gives the note of the next verse.

- At the end, the head of the tigerbox is beaten once and scraped.

- The Emperor then leaves to the Guiding March.'

The Guiding March

+ = drums and castanets

Hymn to Confucius (one verse)

Ta   tsai   Kung   tsu   Hsien   chuch hsien chih

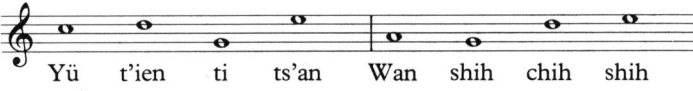

Yü   t'ien   ti   ts'an   Wan   shih   chih   shih

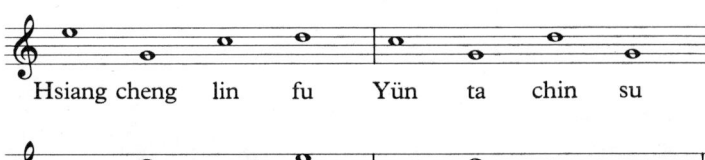

Hsiang cheng lin   fu   Yün   ta   chin   su

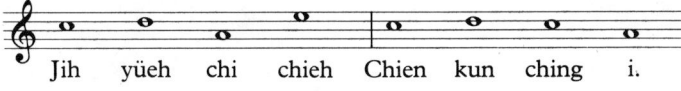

Jih   yüeh   chi   chieh   Chien   kun   ching   i.

Play very slowly on chimes, handbells, tunable drums, zithers, etc., with gongs, sticks and cymbals.

Two poems about Chinese music

Blind men, blind men
In the courtyard of Chou.
We have set up the crossboard, the stand
With the upright hooks, the standing plumes
The little and big drums for beating
The tambourines and stone chimes, the mallet box and
scraper
All is ready and they play.
Panpipes and flutes are ready and begin
Sweetly blend their tones,
Solemn the melody of their bird music.
The ancestors are listening;
As our guests they have come,
To gaze long upon victories.
(*The Book of Songs*, tr. Waley)

The musicians have gone.
The lilacs which they placed
   in the vases of jade
   bend towards the lutes
   and seem to listen still.
(Chang Wu Kien)

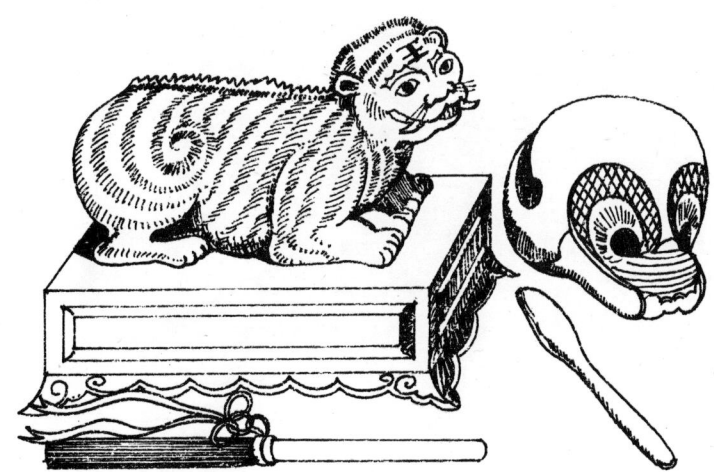

The yü or tiger box: on its back are 27 saw-like teeth. The head is banged, the teeth are scraped.
The mu-yü is a skull-shaped percussion block.

9

Japan

Japanese music has also become very Westernized. Japan has symphony orchestras and international concert artists of great repute, but it is still possible to hear real Japanese music and there is a determined effort on the part of many Japanese to preserve their own traditions.

Japanese music is particularly connected with various kinds

Noh

Bunraku

Kabuki

of theatre. There are three main forms – 'noh', 'bunraku' and 'kabuki'.

Noh plays use just a flute and three drums. The actors sing all the time and are accompanied by the smaller drums. The flute and large drum play in interludes. The plays do not have much action but, to the initiated, they are full of very deep emotion.

The *bunraku* are puppet plays with a singing story teller accompanied by a shamisen. The singing is mixed with all kinds of shouting, weeping, animal noises, etc., to help tell the story vividly.

The *kabuki* plays use music for the various moods of the play. The main instrument is the shamisen plus a great deal of percussion. There are very precise ways of illustrating the moods of the play and the actual location of the scene – just as there are in our film music (see *Music and You*).

Apart from theatre music, the Japanese play their music at home and they also have a ceremonial palace music (gagaku) played by a fairly large ensemble on special occasions.

Japanese music uses a wide variety of scales—some five note and some seven note, all in different combinations of tones and semitones.

Here are some of them:

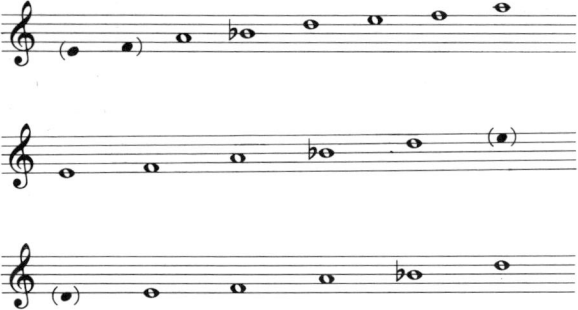

Try making up a song or a piece with one of these scales, or lay out the appropriate chime bars and improvise.

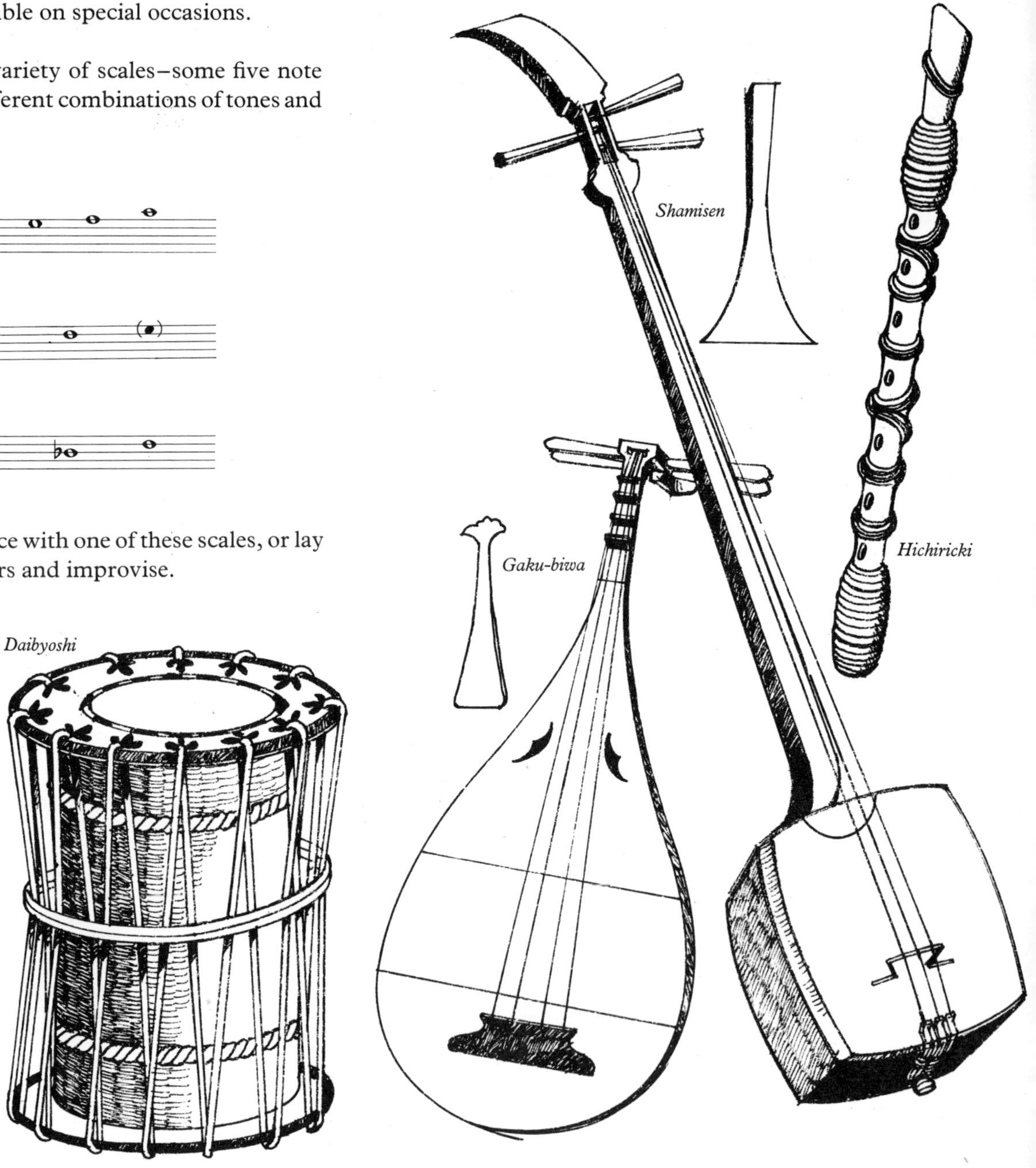

Daibyoshi

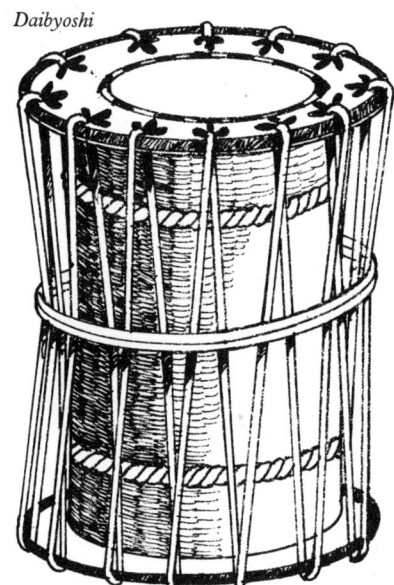

Shamisen

Hichiricki

Gaku-biwa

Indonesia

The principal element in Indonesian music is the 'gamelan' – an orchestra of melodic percussion instruments supplemented in certain areas by a flute, a zither, a two-stringed violin and drums.

The two main styles are those of Java and Bali. The Javanese is slow and stately, the Balinese more lively and colourful; it also uses instruments in two different tunings which makes for a clangorous, shimmering effect.

The music is built up over a basis of long notes played on the largest instruments; the smaller ones playing faster variations above. Gongs punctuate the music at set intervals; the biggest gong is used only at the end of a section, before a new theme is begun.

The scales are usually pentatonic – the steps of the scale are appropriately named ding, dong, deng, dung, dang – but the notes are not exactly like ours. For example, in a scale like this, the G is a bit higher than ours and the other notes are a bit lower.

These ideas might be the basis for a gamelan-type improvisation you could do on chime bars, glockenspiels, etc.

Here is a long, stately tune to play on deep instruments or to sing.

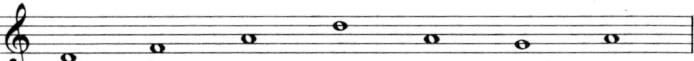

Now play the same notes much faster and in varying patterns over the top.

And add another part on top of that.

This is how gamelan music is built up.

A gamelan orchestra

13

*Katakali is the traditional dance-drama of Southern India.
It consists mainly of chanted, mimed and danced stories from the
ancient Hindu sacred texts—Ramayana and Mahabharata.
The musical accompaniment is supplied by drums, cymbals and
gongs. As with many Eastern music-theatre forms, the separate
parts are almost indivisible; the violent colours of the makeup
of the gods, red, green, white, violet; the enormous collars and
golden head-dresses, the bulky skirted costumes, the stylized
movement and gestures, eyebrow flutterings, ferocious battles
symbolized by a bird-like circular dance, the battery of drums
and gongs, vocal swoops, mimicry of animals in sound and
gesture, all form part of a single but many-sided experience.*

*Another source of music in South-East Asia is the puppet
plays. Shadow puppets are a very popular entertainment. A
few travelling showmen with a whole collection of shadow
puppets will travel from village to village giving performances
of famous legends and myths.*
*All through the performance there is raucous music on an oboe-
type reed instrument and drums. Sometimes the performances
last all day.*

Things to do

● Read from *The Epic of Gilgamesh*—one of the
first accounts of how the world began. Make
some of it into dance or drama with music.

● Listen to Milhaud's *La Création du Monde*.

● Experiment with ways of singing the Psalms
from rhythmic speech to fully musical
settings. Listen to Gregorian chant, Anglican
chant, Stravinsky's *Symphony of Psalms* and
Mass, Britten's setting of Psalm 150, etc.

● Find some records of Indian classical music to
listen to and look out for Indian folk music
and modern Indian and Pakistani popular
music on television and even in your area.

● Read Chinese and Japanese legends about how
music began (see Sachs' *The Rise of Music in
the Ancient World*). Listen to (or go to see)
adaptations of Japanese music drama—
Britten's church parables—*Curlew River*, *The
Prodigal Son*, etc., Weill's *Der Jasager*. Set a
Japanese poem to music using one of the
Japanese scales.

● Find out how to make shadow puppets—there
are several booklets on it—and produce a play
with music for Christmas or Easter.

2 · Europe

Ancient and Modern Greece

The Greeks, like the Chinese, wrote a great deal about the theory of music but the music itself has virtually disappeared and we have very little idea what it was like. Some people find great similarity between the scales of Greek music and those of certain Eastern countries like Japan but we know nothing for certain.

Their main instruments were the *lyre*–played by amateurs for ballad singing and folksongs, the *kithara*–used by professionals for the singing of great poetry and to accompany stage plays, and the *aulos* (a double oboe)–used for virtuoso display and to generate excitement at some of the wilder celebrations of the wine god Dionysus. According to the apparent tuning of the kithara, the Greeks also used a five-note scale but you could alter the notes by pinching the string near its end.

Music was used extensively in Greek drama. The actors chanted all their lines in what was almost operatic style and the aulos was used to add atmosphere. The original performances may well have been rather like some of the Japanese types of drama.

Modern Greece has some of the most exciting music of Europe. Its special feature is its use of time signatures like $\frac{7}{8}$ and $\frac{5}{8}$–these can be thought of as 3 plus 4 beats and 2 plus 3 beats in a bar and are fascinating rhythms to work with.

A vase of c. *490 B.C. depicting a lyre player.*

Kalamatianos

(The Greek national dance, with words and steps)

Come on— now Ha - ra - lam - bi, Get

up out of— your bed No— time to lose—Ha-ra-

-lam - bi It's time for you to wed.

I don't want— her You must take her

I would ra-ther eat and drink all day.—

You can't make— me That's as may be

You had best do what we say.————

I would ra-ther drink all day.— That's as may-be

You can't make me We would ra-ther drink all day.—

Rhythm ⟋ etc.

From *Folk Songs of Greece* arranged and translated by Susan and Ted Alevizos. © 1968 Oak Publications, A Division of Embassy Music Corporation, New York. All Rights Reserved. Used by Permission.

STEPS FOR KALAMATIANOS

Dancers stand in a chain, in an arc, holding hands, feet together, toes to the centre.

1–3 On the first beat begin to step to side on right foot turning to left, completing step on third beat.

4–5 Step back on left foot turning back to line of dance.

6 Step to side on right foot turning to face centre of arc.

7 Hop on right foot turning to face line of dance.

1–3 Step on left foot in front of right.

4–5 Step to side on right foot turning towards left.

6–7 Step back on left foot turning back to line of dance.

1–3 Step to side on right foot turning to face centre.

4–5 Step on left foot in front of right to face line of dance.

6–7 Transfer weight of body back to left foot.

1–3 Step to side on left foot turning to face centre.

4–5 Step on right foot in front of left turning back to line of dance.

6–7 Transfer weight of body back to right foot.

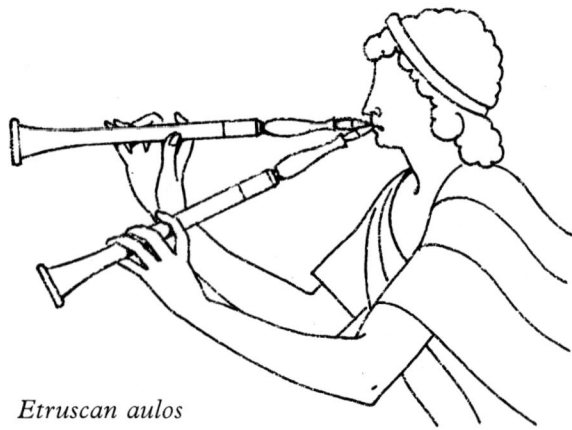

Etruscan aulos

Eastern Europe

The other countries of Eastern Europe—Bulgaria, Jugoslavia, Romania, Russia, etc., are rich in living peasant traditions. Farming is still often unmechanized, peasants spin their own yarn, bake their own bread and observe customs of great antiquity. They also rely largely on their own local and national music for their entertainment. National governments encourage this and send national song and dance teams all over the world to show their traditions. These contain highly trained artists but they do represent a tradition that is still alive in the various countries.

Many interesting survivals of old musical habits can be found in these countries to remind us of the part music played in the lives of our forefathers back in the Middle Ages and before.

In Jugoslavia, you can still hear the singing of *epic ballads*—long poems about past heroes and great battles like those of Ulysses and Beowulf. The Jugoslav singers sing these long poems from memory and never falter over some thousands of lines.

Dancing and singing are combined as they used to be in much earlier days in the West ('ballad' and 'carol' meant 'dance-song' originally). A leader sings a verse, the other dancers sing the refrain.

The dance patterns are the most ancient too—circles and snaking, follow-my-leader lines. Another old feature is the fact that there are men's dances and women's dances and they do not mix very often.

The solitary music of a shepherd or goatherd with his home-made pipe, exploring the sounds of his instrument and producing every kind of trill and ornament is another hint to us of what the earliest unwritten music of our own country was probably like.

Of course, Eastern Europe has not escaped Western

far left: *A folk song and dance company entertaining local shepherds in Kanzakhstan.*

left: *A peasant playing a home-made guale.*

clockwise: *Hungarian State Opera House, Budapest;*
Antonin Dvořák; Krzysztof Penderecki; Frédéric Chopin;
Dmitri Shostakovich; Bedřich Smetana;
Aram Khachaturian.

influences in its music as in all other aspects of its culture. Poland and Czechoslovakia were Roman Catholic countries from an early stage and had Western-style church music. Bohemia (Western Czechoslovakia) produced several fine symphonic writers in the eighteenth century and Mozart himself had many successful engagements in Prague.

In the nineteenth century Eastern Europe was very anxious to imitate the West and produced as many fine composers in the classical styles as any other area—Dvořák, Tchaikovsky, Rimsky-Korsakov and, in our own century, Bartók, Janáček, Shostakovich, Penderecki, Ligeti and many more.

Some of our finest instrumentalists, singers and dancers come from Eastern Europe and opera, concerts and ballet are more popular there than in most European countries. Jazz and rock have been accepted too. In fact, everything you can hear in the West, you can hear in the East, from Prague to Vladivostock. And yet only a short ride out of town will still take you to villages where the music, the instruments and the ceremonies have changed little in three or four hundred years.

Christmas Day Mass in a Russian monastery – 6 January 1973

I set off in a taxi out of Moscow to the Monastery of the Old Believers on the outskirts of the city. The taxi-driver was a bit reluctant to take me there, which I could not quite understand since it was the Russian Orthodox Christmas Day, but when I crossed the stretch of snow-covered waste ground with its scattering of sparse birch trees and arrived in front of the gilded domes of the monastery I think I understood why.

There was a collection of beggars, old men and women, some of them crippled, waiting to receive Christmas gifts of eggs, fruit and money, outside the church. They were probably from the nearby village, like the peasant choir who were to sing inside, but as beggars, in a Socialist Republic, they were not supposed to exist.

In the main church there were hundreds of people. The air was thick with the smell of sweat, Russian soap, candlefat and incense. The inside of the church was mainly brown with four great square pillars holding up the central onion dome. Almost every available space was covered with paintings or icons. At the far end of the church, in front of the altar which one could only partially see, was the 'iconostasis' or 'wall of icons'. Here the most precious holy images were displayed and from two openings in it the priests and monks officiating in the service emerged.

I arrived at nine in the morning when the service had obviously been going on for some time and I left at midday when it was still going on.

The service itself was very active and, although the priests conducted most of the action with processions of sacred books and objects, readings, intonings, etc., the congregation was also involved. They crossed themselves violently and rhythmically in multiples of three, sometimes never stopping, sometimes bowing their heads to the floor, and sang the response to the great antiphons of the Orthodox liturgy.

The intoned 'reading' from the Bible was, I found, the most remarkable musical experience. The priest with his long black hair, huge beard and glittering robes, sang verses from the Bible on one note, as in our psalm-chanting and then slowly rose a semitone or even a quarter tone, in a series of very gradual and almost imperceptible steps. One's ears became keenly attuned to this slow movement upwards – I suppose it has parallels with the movement of incense and spiritual ascent – so that when the final note is reached the sense of resolution and release makes a great climax.

Half-way through the morning a mixed peasant choir, mostly dressed in embroidered white clothes and scarves came into the central body of the church to sing special Christmas hymns. They did not have individual copies of the music but one of the choir held up an enormous book on which great square notes of the hymn appeared. The leader of the group conducted with a three-foot long baton, almost seeming to point at the notes.

It was like being flung back to the Middle Ages, I had seen pictures like this in illuminated manuscripts and here it was going on not five miles from the Russian Space Museum and Exhibition of Twentieth Century Technology.

(I.B.)

Things to do

● Collect pictures and photographs of instruments and dances from Eastern Europe.

● Find out what are the traditional instruments of Poland, Bulgaria, Romania, Jugoslavia, Hungary – and what their music is like. Try to trace at least one song from each country.

● Listen to:
Bartók's 'Rumanian Dances'
Kodály's *Dances of Galanta*
Janáček's 'Children's Songs'
Shostakovich's Violin Concerto
Enesco's 'Rumanian Rhapsody'
Dvořák's 'Slavonic Dances'

Western Europe

The music of Western Europe has been written about over and over again in countless histories of music. This section will try to avoid covering the same ground but will rather deal with the subject from a different angle. It will look less at composers and pieces of music and more at the *uses* to which music has been put in our society. These will be dealt with under three main headings:

music for official purposes—church, court, city and state
private recreation
public entertainment

3 · Official Music

The Church

The basic music of the Roman Catholic Church (which formerly covered all Western Europe) is Gregorian or Roman chant—a whole body of tunes for every service and feast of the Church. This music has now been in use for a thousand years with little change. There is no harmony and the rhythm is that of the words themselves. The tunes use a fairly small range of notes but listened to in the setting of one of the great Gothic cathedrals they are most inspiring.

Some chants are simple and familiar enough for congregations to join in. For special festivals there are more elaborate chants which only a choir can manage ... 'Alleluia' is a favourite word for these more difficult passages.

The main cathedrals had expert choirs run by a choirmaster and organist who was usually a skilled composer too (see *Music and Musicians*). Often the King considered the principal cathedral of his country his own church and the choir members his servants. He maintained what was called a 'chapel'—this does not mean a building but a group of musicians—singers and players—in the service of the church or court. The king's musicians were called the Chapel Royal. We still have one in this country consisting of the singers employed in the various royal churches—Westminster, Hampton Court, Windsor, St James', St Paul's.

In the old days members of the Chapel Royal would accompany the King on foreign visits and wars. Henry V had his singers with him to sing Mass throughout his campaigns in France. An old poem of the time says that, at the capture of Rouen in 1419,

> Hys chapylle mette him at the doore
> And went by foore him in the floore
> And songe a respond gloryus.

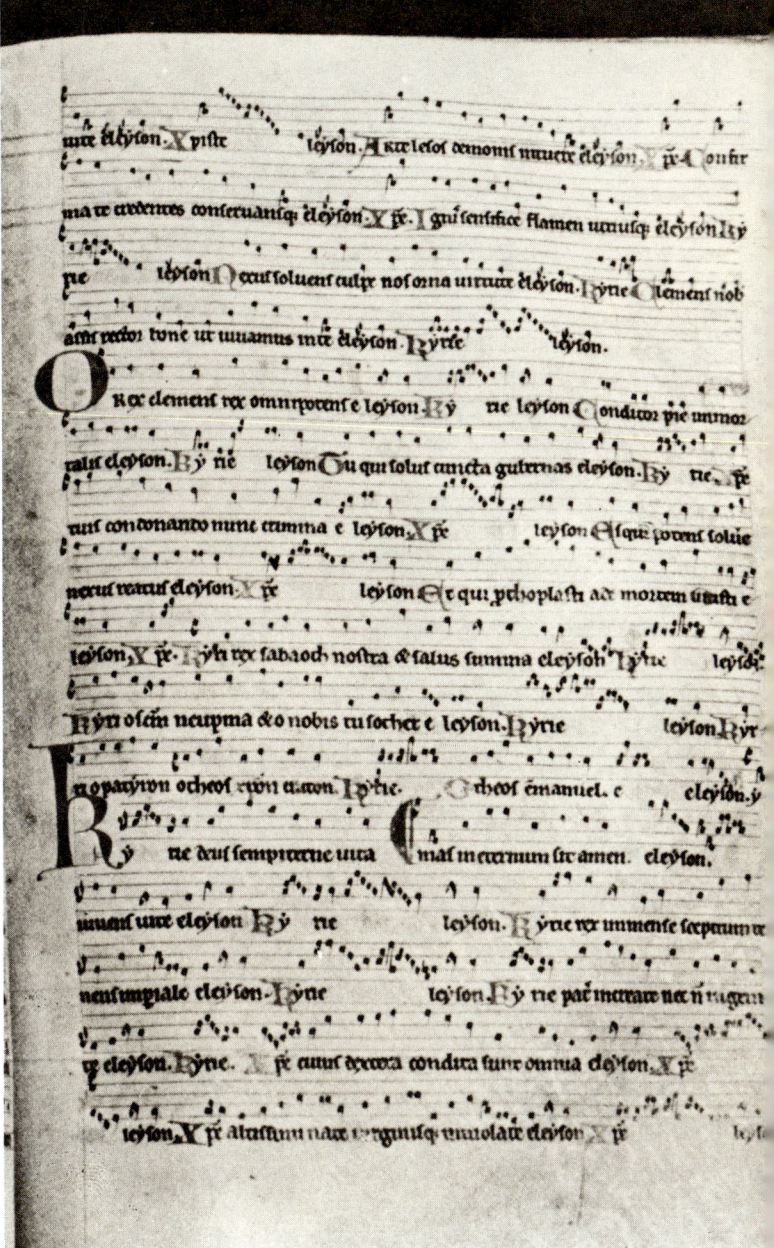

Gregorian chant, a type of plainsong associated with Pope Gregory I.

right: *Title page of* Theatrum Instrumentorum seu Sciagraphia, *a mass for three choirs by Michael Praetorius.*

far right: *Thomas Tallis*

As composers became more expert and music more complicated, Church music in the big churches at important festivals became very professional and the service was almost a concert. There were complaints about this and at one point the Pope stepped in and said composers and choirs should not show off so much and should make their pieces simpler so that the congregation could at least follow the words even if they could not join in.

There were some simpler kinds of Church music even at this time. St Francis of Assissi wanted people to be able to sing praises to God without the help of expert choirs. He encouraged people to make up religious folksongs called 'laude' (singular 'lauda') which he and his followers sang on their pilgrimages and at gatherings. Our old English carols are a similar attempt on the part of some priests to give people simpler religious music.

The hymns we sing nowadays in churches and chapels were first written at the beginning of the Reformation around 1500. The German religious leader Luther was one of the first hymn-writers–he was a musician as well as a priest–and he encouraged others in his movement to write tunes and words as well. They wanted everyone to join in the music at services. The words were mainly from psalms set in rhyme–the tunes were folk-tunes or even old plainsong tunes but sung more rhythmically. The earliest English hymn-writers were Tallis and Gibbons and in France and Switzerland the new Protestant believers sang the psalm arrangements of Louis Bourgeois and Claude Goudimel.

Hymn-writing continued in England into the seventeenth, eighteenth and nineteenth centuries with such well-known writers as Isaac Watts and Charles Wesley. The Puritans used folksongs for tunes and took many of them with them to America where they are still sung by remote Southern communities. The Methodist movement and the Salvation Army started a new tradition of really rousing hymns, almost like community songs, drawing especially on the American collection *Sacred Songs and Solos* compiled by Ira Sankey. More recently there has been yet another move to integrate folk and popular-style tunes into religious worship with the songs of writers like Sydney Carter and others.

An 'Allelula'

Al- le- -- -- -- lu- ia -- -- -- -- -- -- -a -- -- -- -- -- --

A lauda

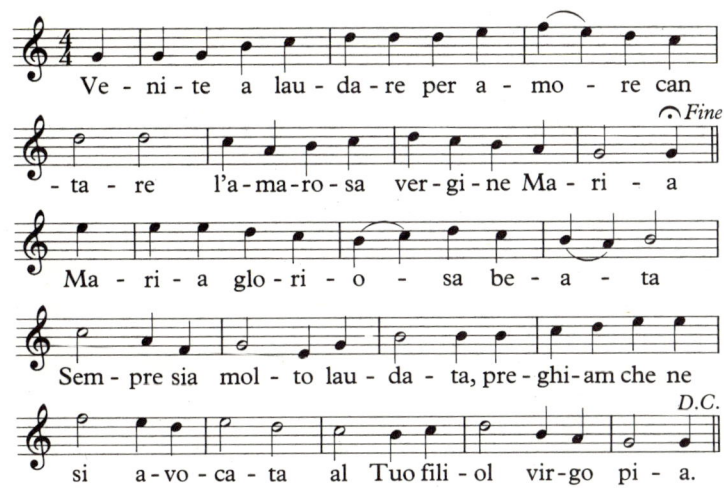

Ve- ni- te a lau- da- re per a- mo- re can-

Fine

-ta- re l'a- ma- ro- sa ver- gi- ne Ma- ri- a

Ma- ri- a glo- ri- o- sa be- a- ta

Sem- pre sia mol- to lau- da- ta, pre- ghi- am che ne

D.C.

si a- vo- ca- ta al Tuo fili- ol vir- go pi- a.

Look at:
'King Herod and the Cock'
'The Cherry Tree Carol'
'Dives and Lazarus'
in *The Oxford Book of Carols*

See *Spiritual Folksongs of Early America* and *White Spirituals in the Southern Uplands*, both by G. Pullen-Jackson; also *A Treasury of American Song*, by O. Downes and E. Siegmeister

A Puritan hymn to an old folk-tune

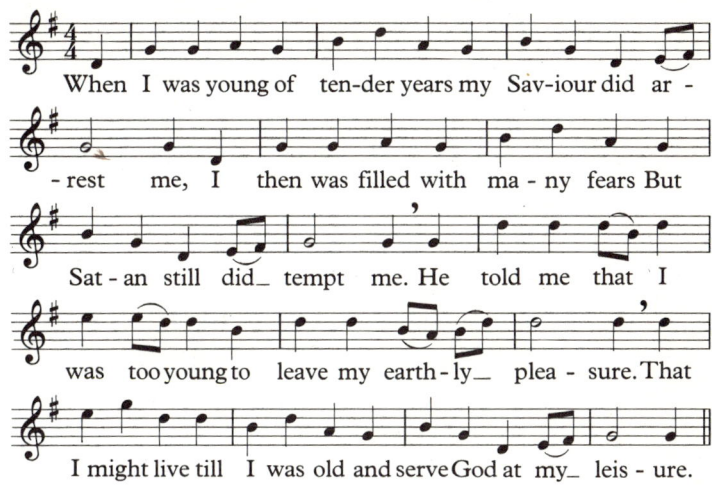

When I was young of ten-der years my Sav-iour did ar-

-rest me, I then was filled with ma-ny fears But

Sat-an still did_ tempt me. He told me that I

was too young to leave my earth-ly_ plea-sure. That

I might live till I was old and serve God at my_ leis-ure.

A STIRRING CAMP MEETING SONG

Bound for the Promised Land

On Jor- dan's stor- my banks I stand And

cast a wish- ful eye To Ca- naan's fair and

hap- py land where my pos- se- ssions

lie. I am bound for the pro-mised land _____ I'm

bound for the pro-mised land O_____ who will come and

go with me. I am bound for the pro-mised land.

Count your Blessings

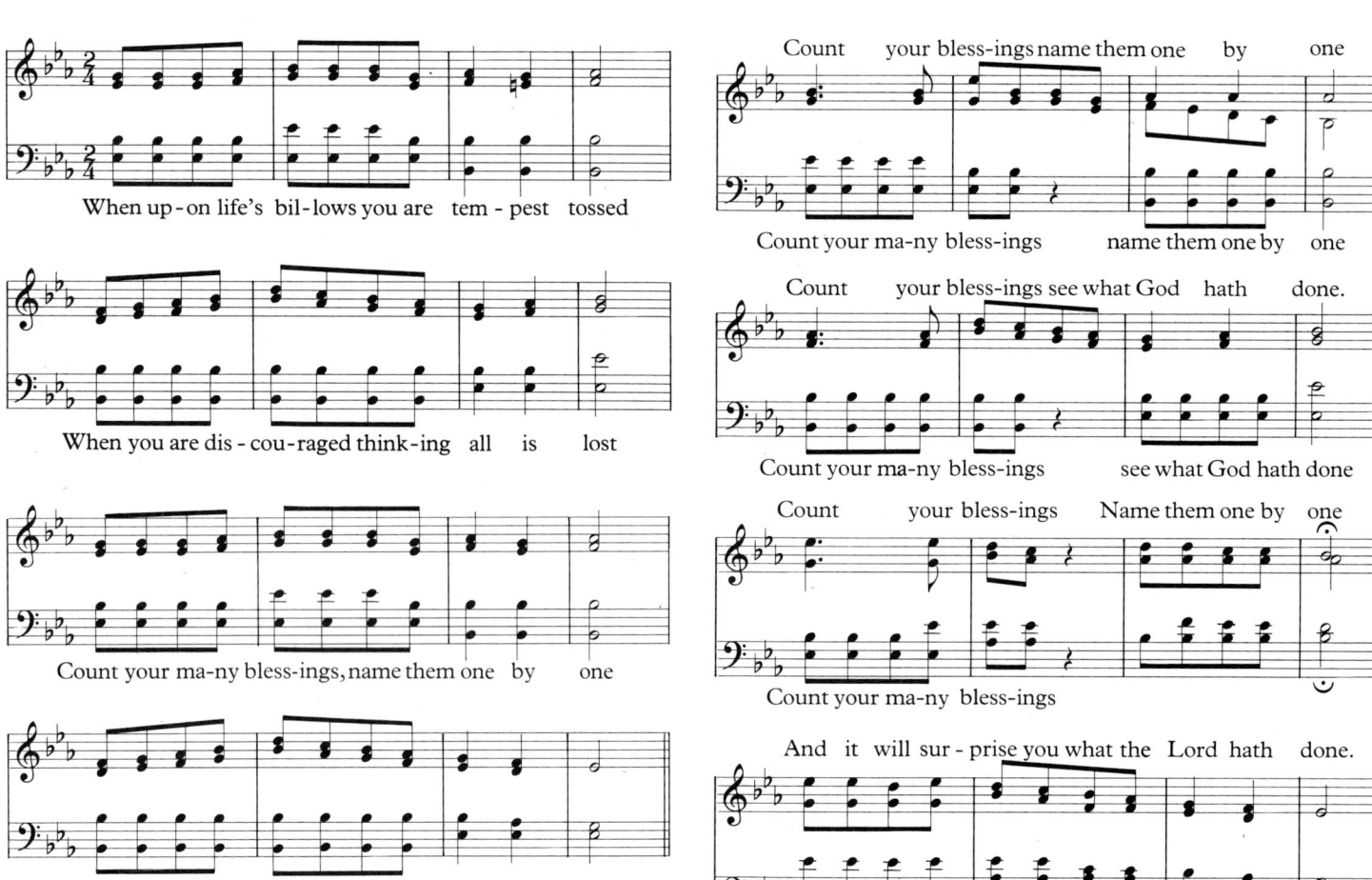

When up-on life's bil-lows you are tem - pest tossed

When you are dis - cou-raged think-ing all is lost

Count your ma-ny bless-ings, name them one by one

And it will sur-prise you what the Lord hath done.

Count your bless-ings name them one by one

Count your ma-ny bless-ings name them one by one

Count your bless-ings see what God hath done.

Count your ma-ny bless-ings see what God hath done

Count your bless-ings Name them one by one

Count your ma-ny bless-ings

And it will sur - prise you what the Lord hath done.

The elaborate 'concert' music continued to be written and performed in the big churches at special festivals and still is today, though less often as a part of a service, more likely as a definite performance. Long, complex and thrilling arrangements of the various sections of the Mass for large choirs and orchestras have been written by Bach, Haydn, Mozart, Beethoven, Stravinsky, Bruckner, Schubert and many others. The Mass for the Dead (Requiem Mass) has inspired the most awe-inspiring music of Berlioz, Verdi and Britten.

PROCESSIONS AND PAGEANTS

Noisy, colourful processions are still an important part of religious festivals in many countries, especially Spain and Spanish America. They used to be just as popular in Northern Europe in the Middle Ages with music from choirboys and waits much in evidence. Plays were done too on religious subjects – first of all actually in the church though later mainly outside in the market place. These gave plenty of scope for

Celebrating Corpus Christi in Granada.

music too—angel choirs, shepherd pipes, trumpets on the Day of Judgment, etc. The towns of Coventry and York often revive their 'mystery plays' and in Spain and Mexico they are still traditionally performed. The climax of this tradition came with a super-colossal spectacle called *La Rappresentazione di Anima e di Corpo* ('The body and soul show') with music by Cavalieri produced in Rome in 1600 with song, dance, mime, orchestra and spectacular scenic effects. After that, we had to wait for *Godspell, Jesus Christ Superstar* and Ellington's *Genesis* to take up the idea again.

above: *A York mystery play*

right: *Rappresentazione di Anima e di Corpo*

Court music

In the days when kings and queens and other nobles had to show off their wealth and power in order to impress their subjects and rivals, music was a great status symbol. All rulers and many other members of the aristocracy employed their own personal bands of musicians and a director to rehearse them and compose all the necessary music. Some noble masters were accomplished musicians themselves—Henry VIII wrote pleasant pieces, Maria Teresa of Austria was a fine singer, Frederick the Great of Prussia preferred playing the flute to court business.

Royal weddings (often political arrangements) and state visits were the occasions that called for impressive musical displays. Even today, it is customary for visiting royalty and diplomats to attend the opera or ballet (rather than the theatre or concert hall). In the days of the great monarchs, a specially conceived entertainment would be laid on in the palace or castle. In the sixteenth century these would be lavish displays of song, dance, mime, poetry, splendid costume and scenic effects—fountains, artificial forests, flying gods, earthquakes, monsters—a whole fantasy world of the old Greek myths and legends they loved so much, brought to life. The earlier shows were called 'ballets' (though they were not just dancing) or 'masques'. Later, in the seventeenth and eighteenth centuries, they were called operas or opera-ballets and music gradually became more and more important.

Military music in the courtyard of St James's Palace c. 1790.

27

Ballet Comique: La Grande Entrée

Arrange this for your orchestra or class.

28

LE BALLET COMIQUE DE LA REINE

Performed in Paris on 15 October, 1581 to celebrate the marriage of the Duc de Joyeuse to Mlle de Vaudemont—the queen's half-sister.

Part of the producer's description:

Outside the garden on either side were two vaulted trellises fifteen feet long and twenty-four high, with leaves and fine grapes which appeared natural. This place was the more remarkable because through it must pass the musicians for the intermedii and the vehicles which were to appear before the King. Now this garden was the place where Circe the enchantress had her abode. She was seated in the gate of the castle, clad in a golden robe of two colours, decorated all over with small tufts of gold and silk and she wore a veil of silver and silk crepe; the adornments of her head and arms being marvellously enriched with precious stones and pearls of inestimable worth. . . . She lived, as we have said, in this garden where there were a hundred wax candles, emitting such light, shining so upon the fairy and the garden, that the eyes of the spectators were dazzled. In addition the infinity of tapers which were at the top and all around the room gave forth such a brilliant light as to put to shame the finest and calmest day of the year . . .

When their Majesties, princes, princesses, lords and ladies, kings, ambassadors and foreign princes had been seated in the chairs and places prepared for each, according to his rank . . . one heard from behind the castle the sound of oboes, trumpets, sackbuts and other sweet musical instruments. When their harmony had ceased, Lord de la Roche (a gentleman serving the Queen Mother, clad in silver cloth, his garment covered with precious stones and pearls)— Lord de la Roche, coming from Circe's garden, ran into the middle of the room.

Final song from the Festivities for the marriage of Cosimo I of Florence, 1539

The opera *Pomo d'Oro* by Cesti

A shining machine appeared, as if touched with gold, out of a few rent-opened clouds, made with singular art. And, breaking away completely from the sky, it came to the ground without permitting the eye to penetrate to its supports. Upon it sat Justice with a Lion and, by her side, a sword, scales in her hand, clothed in a blue coat sprinkled with gold, rich and beautiful above manner. A valorous castrato from Rome took the part who gained great applause for noble and stately gestures in a noteworthy performance.

Then, from the right of the sea, arose a car in the form of a golden shell drawn by sea-horses which moved from the right to the centre of the stage, turned round and stopped facing the body of the theatre. This car bore Neptune king of the waves, surrounded by his Tritons, excellently played. He was entirely naked except for a beautiful rich blue and gold cloak which covered him in some parts. A tenor from Parma took the part gaining praise and giving wonderful satisfaction to the audience.

At his command a most exquisite and life-like model of Venice arose from the sea which everyone confessed to be a *tour de force*. The eye was deceived by the Piazza and public buildings which were imitated to the life and it rejoiced more hourly as it forgot that the entertainment came from a concealment of the truth. . . .

The prologue, a great pledge and trial of the whole drama being finished, six soldiers, eight halberdiers and four pages of King Ariobarte, servants of his chief captain Paristide, came from the principal gate of the city in long file and went toward the pier to meet his daughter the widowed Queen of Argos. The soldiers were armed with cuirasses and helmets with blue plumes. They wore blue stockings, a livery trimmed with great golden roses, skirts of gold lace, sashes of blue and gold crepe from which hung their swords, and gold buskins on their feet. Their captain wore rich armour encrusted with jewels, a blue sash, plume and smart looking half-boots. The halberdiers were dressed as janissaries with undercoats of red and gold with surcoats of blue to their feet with ruffles, great collars in the Greek style, lined with beautifully coloured cloth, trimmed with gold, and janissary berets with falling plumes matching the surcoats. Sashes of

cloth of gold held their scimitars. And in their hands they bore very evil lances. The pages were dressed entirely in silver, full breeches (bragoni interi) half-boots and Polish berets with silver plumes. On their shoulders they had coats open at the neck in front, with half-sleeves, blue at the sides and lined with cloth of red and gold with gold lacings. These *comparse* gave amazing pleasure. And the audience admitted that a royal court could not have arranged it with greater propriety and beauty.

SOME ROYAL OCCASIONS AND THEIR MUSIC

1364   Coronation of Charles V of France
       Mass setting–G. de Machault

1666   Wedding of Leopold I of Austria with the Infanta
       Margerita of Spain
       The Golden Apple; opera–Cesti (see above.)

1694   Funeral of Queen Mary
       'Thou Knowest Lord' and brass music–Purcell

1685   Coronation of James II
       'My Heart is Inditing'–Purcell

1727   Coronation of George II
       'Zadok the Priest'–Handel

1791   Coronation of Leopold II of Bohemia
       La clemenza di Tito; opera–Mozart

1953   Coronation of Elizabeth II
       Te Deum–Walton

City and state

The councils of towns and the governments of republics also call on musicians to enhance special occasions. The Town Waits (see *Music and Musicians*) were paid by the corporation to be on hand to welcome distinguished visitors and to play for processions, fairs, civic celebrations, receptions, weddings and funerals of important citizens. Many German towns had a full-time Music Director—Bach held the post in Leipzig. In England this does not happen, these functions are usually shared between various officials—the Cathedral Organist, the Music Adviser, the local university professor—and there is not in fact a great deal of civic music except through the schools, colleges and churches, and where there is a city orchestra as in Liverpool, Birmingham, Bournemouth and Manchester.

State music, as opposed to court music, appeared at the time of the French Revolution. The leaders of the Republic realized the value of assemblies for the people to promote a sense of unity and loyalty. Open-air demonstrations with patriotic speeches were frequently held in the big cities, and revolutionary hymns and marching songs were supplied by composers of the day—Méhul, Gossec, Lesueur, Cherubini—for everyone to join in to the accompaniment of large military bands. Berlioz wrote his *Symphonie funèbre et triomphale* for a civic commemoration parade at a slightly later date.

Even opera was political. Many composers were in sympathy with anti-royalist and nationalist movements in the nineteenth century and wrote operas on this theme. Mozart's *Marriage of Figaro* could be considered the first, followed by *Fidelio* (Beethoven), *Les Huguenots* (Meyerbeer), *Sicilian Vespers* (Verdi).

Verdi was a national hero in Italy at the time of their fight for unification and his operas were often the scenes of political demonstration. Nowadays, music has less political significance except in Communist countries like the Soviet Union and China. Here, however, music is considered a very important aspect of politics and composers are expected to write music that supports the political ideas of the state; not so different, in fact, from the days when composers were employed to write in support of the Church or the ruling monarch.

In the West, governments do not ask for special music very often—only perhaps for some anniversary or the opening of a new hall or college. Some music was commissioned for the opening of the Severn Bridge. The United Nations commissioned an anthem. Apart from that sort of thing, the only new state music one comes across is among new nations like those of Africa where it can still help to strengthen a sense of community.

SOME FAMOUS CIVIL COMMISSIONS

1692   Ode for St Cecilia's Day   Purcell
City banquet on St Cecilia's Day

1840   *Symphonie funèbre et triomphale*   Berlioz
Inauguration of Bastille Column

1871   *Aida*   Verdi
Opening of Suez Canal

1873   Requiem   Verdi
Death of Manzoni

1930   *Job*   Vaughan Williams
Norwich Festival

1947   'Flourish all powerful land'   Prokofiev
30th anniversary of the Revolution

1962   *War Requiem*   Britten
Opening of Coventry Cathedral

1970   *Poème électronique*   Varèse
Expo 70

1971   *Mass*   Bernstein
Opening of Kennedy Center

Find more commissions to add to these.

Things to do

● Think up a masque-type entertainment or a pageant like the ones described, to do at:
  The opening of a new school
  Speech Day
  The opening of a new supermarket or motorway
  United Nations Day
  School leavers' last day
For the music you can use well-known records—or put new words to current hits.

● Write a new national anthem for this country—or for your own county, city or town.

● Write a national anthem for Mars.

● Listen to 'Hymnen' by Karlheinz Stockhausen, a medley of national anthems in many different disguises.

4 · Private Recreation

Folk music

Most folk-dance and folksong in Europe is now deliberately preserved by interested groups who give displays to tourists and meet to show their traditions at annual festivals. Urban growth, easy travel and mechanical reproduction have all contributed to make folk music less spontaneously alive in country districts.

Strangely enough two of the most urbanized countries—England and America—have seen a terrific growth in popularity of folk music over recent years and many aspects of British and American folk music have been absorbed into the popular music of today.

FOLK-DANCE

England has some of the oldest traditions of dance in the Morris dances of the Cotswolds and the sword dances of the North East. The name 'Morris' probably derived from

left: *Modern Morris dancers;* above: *as depicted on a stained glass window.*

'Moorish' and an old dance called 'La Moresca' which was a mock fight between Moors and Christians; some dances still include mock fencing with sticks. The fool, the hobby horse, the green man and the man dressed as a woman are the relics of old pagan representations of nature gods.

The sword dances probably came from Scandinavia—they were associated with sun worship and with the death and resurrection theme of the mumming plays which they often introduce.

Mixed dancing is of later origin. Early mixed dances were in circles or serpentine lines as in the 'conga' and Greek dance. A line of women facing a line of men is an adaptation of the

Trunkles, a Morris tune

Bavarian Ländler

aristocratic couple dances that began in the Middle Ages. Many of the dances that are called 'country' dances are not from the country at all. They are genteel indoor dances of the seventeenth century first presented in a book called *The Dancing Master* published by John Playford in 1650. Dances from the country villages are more accurately called 'community dances' and should be done very vigorously and even noisily.

The other countries of Northern Europe have mainly couple dances in waltz or march rhythms in which the couple remain the same all the time—people do not change partners so much. This was one of the attractions of the waltz when it was first introduced to England in the nineteenth century, as in most English dances, both in the villages and in the ballroom, one changed partners for each turn of the dance, so it was not so easy to pursue any particular lady very persistently!

The French have the *bourrée* and *basse danse*—relics of old court dances which hung on in the countryside long after the gentry had given them up; they also have many 'farandole'-type dances—the follow-my-leader ones also seen in Greece and Israel which are some of the oldest in Europe. Italian and Spanish dancing show strong gipsy influence with much imitation courtship, the male showing off and the lady alternately accepting and rejecting him.

SONG

Dance and song are not so closely connected in the West as they are in the East, although at some former date they must have been. The words 'carol' and 'ballad' both meant dance-song originally.

Now, the word ballad means different things in different musical connections. In folk music, it means a particular kind of medieval story-song with a large number of simple four-line verses often with a refrain in the second and fourth lines.

The Four Maries

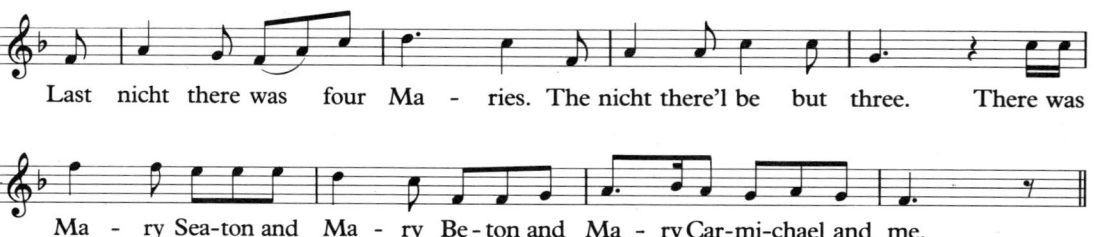

Last nicht there was four Ma - ries. The nicht there'l be but three. There was
Ma - ry Sea-ton and Ma - ry Be-ton and Ma - ry Car-mi-chael and me.

1. Word's gone to the kitchen and word's gone to the hall
   That Mary Hamilton gangs wi' bairn to the highest Stewart of all.

2. He's courted her in the kitchen, he's courted her in the hall
   He's courted her in the low cellar and that was worst of all!

3. She's tied it to her apron and she's thrown it in the sea
   Says Sink ye swim ye bonny wee babe You'll ne'er get more o' me.

4. Down then came the old queen, gold tassels tying her hair
   O Mary where's the bonny wee babe that I heard greet so sair.

5. There was never a babe intill my room as little designs to be
   It was but a touch o' my sair side come o'er my fair body.

6. O Mary put on your robes o' black or else your robes o' brown
   For ye maun go wi' me tonight to see fair Edinbro' town.

7. I winna put on my robes o' black nor yet my robes o' brown
   But I'll put on my robes o' white to shine through Edinbro' town.

8. When she came up the Cannogate she laugh'd loud laughters three
   But when she came down the Cannogate the tear blinded her ee.

9. When she gaed up the Parliament stair the heel came off her shee
   And lang or she came down again she was condemned to dee.

10. When she came down the Cannogate the Cannogate so free
    Many a lady looked o'er her window Weeping for this lady

11. Ye need na weep for me she says, ye need na weep for me
    For had I not slain mine own sweet babe this death I wouldna dee.

12. Bring me a bottle o' wine she says, the best that e'er ye hae
    That I may drink to my well-wishers and they may drink to me.

13. Here's a health to the jolly sailors that sail upon the main
    Let them never let on to my father and mother but what I'm coming ham.

14. Here's a health to the jolly sailors that sail upon the sea
    Let them never let on to my father and mother that I came here to dee.

15. O little did my mother think when first she cradled me
    What lands I was to travel through what death I was to dee.

16. O little did my father think the day he held up me
    What lands I was to travel through What death I was to dee.

17. Last nicht I was'd the queen's feet and gently laid her down
    And a' the thanks I've gotten the nicht to be hanged in Edinbro' town.

18. Last nicht, etc. . . .

These ballads were particularly widespread in Northern Europe. The English and Scottish ones were collected and classified by an American scholar called Francis Child and are often referred to as the Child Ballads. Many have now been recorded, even by electric bands such as the Fairport Convention and Steeleye Span.

Here are some of the commonest stories—often magical and violent—and the titles of some of the various ballads with that story.

The devil's questions—The devil, or some disguised version of him, asks riddles which the victim has to answer in order to be freed. Later it is a suitor who has to answer the girl's riddles—'The Elfin Knight', 'The False Knight on the Road', 'Scarborough Fair'.

The return of the ghost to its murderer or lover—'The Unquiet Grave', 'The Wife of Usher's Well', 'Sweet William's Ghost', 'Polly Vaughan'.

Infidelity or tragedy in love—'The Lass of Roch Royal', 'Barbara Allen', 'Little Musgrave and Lady Barnard', 'The Gipsy Laddie' (and all its variants), 'Frankie and Johnny' (much later).

Murder of the rival brother (cf. Esau and Jacob)—'Edward my Son', 'Lord Randal', 'The Two Sisters' (rivals for the same man) also called 'The Berkshire Tragedy', 'The Farmer's Daughters', etc.

By the end of the Middle Ages most new popular songs were written in the towns and circulated in the country by pedlars, ballad-sellers and beggar-musicians. Many popular songs, later called folksongs came from plays of the theatre or the market place and others from published collections of songs printed in considerable quantity in the seventeenth century (page 49).

It is worth remembering that a folksong need not be very old—a song remembered by a ninety-year-old man may have been new when he learnt it—nor did they just grow—most of them were written by somebody in the first place, however much people varied them afterwards.

Well Met, Pretty Maid

(From *Thomas and Sally* by T. Arne)

An eighteenth-century operetta and pleasure-garden song, later a broadside and now called a folksong (with different words).

Well met pret - ty maid— Come don't— be— a - fraid— I

mean I— mean no mis-chief I— vow. What is it you ail? Come

give me your pail, and I'll car - ry it up to your cow. What

2 Pray let it alone, I have hands of my own
   No need no need yours to help me. Forbear!
   How can you insist for I will not be kiss'd
   So carry your trifles elsewhere.

3 In yon lovely grove there is an alcove
   All round, all round the sweet violets spring
   And there is a thrush sits by in a bush
   It will charm you to hear how she sing.

4 Hark hark prithee hark! See yonder's a lark
   She warbles, she warbles and pleases me so
   To hear the soft tale of the sweet nightingale
   I will not be tempted to go.

5 Then here we'll sit down. My dear do not frown
   No longer no longer my bliss I'll retard
   Kind Venus shall spread a veil overhead
   And the little rogue Cupid shall guard.

Tavern music

Drink has always been one of music's closest companions. The noise that comes out of your local on Saturday nights may not be very melodious (unless you live in Wales or Cornwall) but the tradition that is being carried on is universal and as old as man himself.

The repertoire of songs for drinking to is never very wide at any one time—in England it is largely the current popular favourites and rude rugby songs; in America it tends to be sentimental Edwardian ballads. French students have a wealth of songs about student life and the Germans actually sing songs about drinking!

The drinking songsters of Elizabethan days seem to have been rather more learned in their material. They sang 'catches'—rounds, that is—and songs in three parts called 'threemen's songs' or 'freemen's songs', many of which were printed and they were often referred to by Shakespeare:

SIR TOBY BELCH But shall we make the welkin dance indeed?
　　Shall we rouse the night-owl in a catch that will draw
　　three souls out of one weaver? shall we do that?

SIR ANDREW AGUECHEEK An you love me, let's do't. I am dog at a catch.

FESTE By 'r lady, sir, and some dogs will catch well.

SIR ANDREW Most certain. Let our catch be, 'Thou knave'.

FESTE 'Hold thy peace, thou knave,' knight? I shall be constrain'd in't to call thee knave, knight.

SIR ANDREW 'Tis not the first time I have constrained one to call me knave.
　　Begin, fool: it begins, 'Hold thy peace'.

Twelfth Night, Act II, Scene III

In the eighteenth century the fashion passed and those who still wanted to sing catches and part-songs (now called 'glees') formed societies and met regularly in their own separate rooms. These were later called 'song and supper rooms' and were used for recitals as well as informal singing.

France too had its 'song cellars' and Germany its *Liederkreis* all centred on drinking houses. The German universities built up their own tradition of drinking parties combined with good, informal choral singing and this tradition was taken to America by German emigrants and eventually gave rise to the famous Yale and Harvard Glee Clubs and their celebrated repertoire of 'student songs'.

'A Catch for the House' by Henry Purcell

Once in our lives let us drink to our wives Tho' their
num-bers be_ but_ small, Heav'n take the best and the
dev-il take the rest. And_ so we shall get rid_ of them
all. To this heart-y wish let each_
man take his dish And drink drink till he fall

The catch from _Twelfth Night_

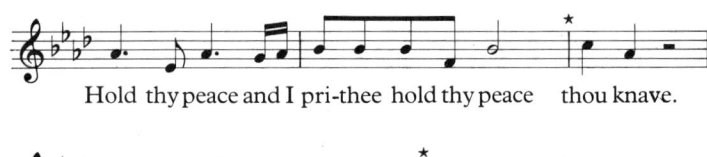

Hold thy peace and I pri-thee hold thy peace thou knave.

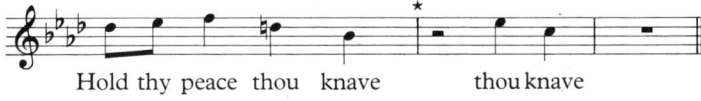

Hold thy peace thou knave thou knave

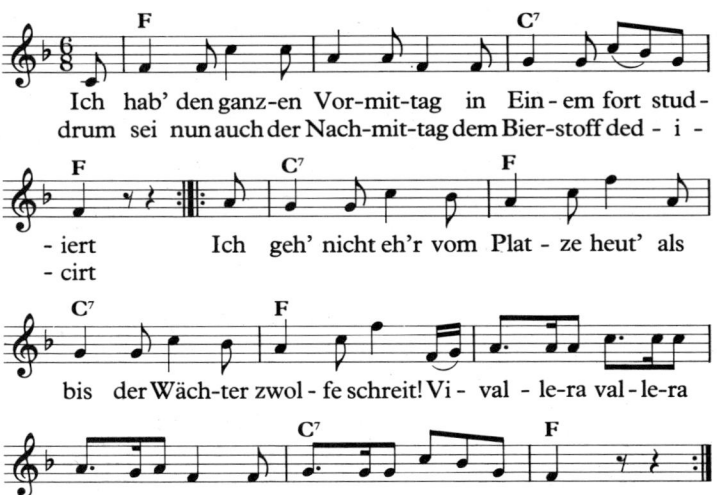

Ich hab' den ganz-en Vor-mit-tag in Ein-em fort stud-
drum sei nun auch der Nach-mit-tag dem Bier-stoff ded-i-
- iert Ich geh' nicht eh'r vom Plat-ze heut' als
- cirt
bis der Wäch-ter zwol-fe schreit! Vi- val-le-ra val-le-ra
val-le-ra la Vi val-le-ra val-le-ra la

Was ist des Lebens höchste Lust
Die Liebe und der Wein.
Wenn's Liebchen ruht an meiner Brust
dünk ich mich Füst zu sein.
Und bei dem edlem Berstensaft
traüm 'ich von Kron' und Kaiserschaft!

Music at home

Music-making at home is bound to be a little more dignified than in a public house—for one thing the company is mixed.

Old paintings often show us ladies and courtiers singing and playing together at home. Music used to be considered a necessary accomplishment for all noble ladies and gentlemen. The ladies played light instruments like the dulcimer, psaltery and 'portative' organ—gentlemen sang to the lute.

Some of the oldest songs we have written out in music are those of the troubadours of the twelfth century—noble men who wrote love lyrics for their ladies which their minstrel servants then set to music.

In the European courts and stately homes of the fifteenth and sixteenth centuries, group singing in parts was as popular a pastime as horseriding. They must have been good readers too—the songs were quite difficult.

Pepys and Evelyn in their famous diaries, often mention home music-making in their day. This was the time of the first serious attempts to print and publish music on a large scale and many of the early publications were tutors for people to learn how to play instruments—along with simple beginners' pieces.

left: *Family concert, 1811;* above: *'The quartet'* by *A. Hendschel;* below: *'Playing in parts'* by *J. Gillray.*

A Duet for Amateurs (on any instruments) by Georg Philipp Telemann

(orig. key B♭)

Although professional concerts increased in the eighteenth century, home music continued. Ladies played the spinet and piano; gentlemen learned the flute or violin. Germany was more active in home music than England at this time. Professional and scholarly men in Germany were particularly fond of instrumental playing at home. Consequently, vast quantities of music for small groups of players were printed in Germany and many amateur music clubs were formed meeting regularly in members' houses. Because of this very active amateur music-making, composers were able to continue to make a living, even after noble patronage was no longer available, by giving lessons, writing pieces for the groups and for individual pianists and others.

Home music revived in England in Victorian times though the music played was not always of the highest quality. It was mainly music for piano and voice, not too difficult, pleasant and tuneful and, in the case of the songs, often rather sentimental or even morbid. It was particularly a pastime of the middle class—the aristocracy were more inclined to pay someone to come and play for them. Chopin, Liszt, Schumann and Mendelssohn were frequently engaged by the wealthy to entertain at private parties.

The Gipsy's Warning (a Victorian parlour song)

Do not trust him gen-tle la-dy Though his voice be low and sweet Heed not him who kneels be-fore thee, Gen-tly plead-ing at thy feet. Now thy life is in it's morn-ing. Cloud not this thy hap-py lot Li-sten to the Gip-sy's warn-ing Gen-tle la-dy trust him not. Li-sten to the Gip-sy's warn-ing Gen-tle la-dy trust him not.

Industrial music

Many of the early factory-owners were concerned over the dullness of their workers' lives and one of their ways of trying to brighten them was to encourage music-making, largely on the basis of the brass band whose instruments had then recently been invented by the Frenchman Adolphe Sax (in the 1840s). There had been bands before this but these new instruments really set the movement going. They were comparatively easy to play, they made a pleasant sound and blended well and if you could play one of them, it took very little time to play any other as they all had more or less the same fingering. The brass-band movement is still strong, especially in industrial areas, and the various regional and national festivals help to keep interest alive and raise standards of playing. A great many people who would never have taken any interest in orchestras or opera have discovered the pleasures of music-making through brass bands.

Closely connected with these are the amateur choral societies that have been, till recently at least, such a feature of English music. They stemmed largely from the Methodist and other non-conformist chapels of the nineteenth century where congregational singing was so lusty. The choirs from these chapels began to tackle larger items—the fashionable oratorios—*Messiah*, *Elijah*, etc., of Victorian times and many grew into very large and expert choral societies. From these came another off-shoot—the male voice choirs of the Welsh and Cornish mining communities—also chapel inspired—and the amateur operatic societies which still flourish in many towns and which stemmed originally from the enormous success of the Gilbert and Sullivan operettas.

A male voice choir

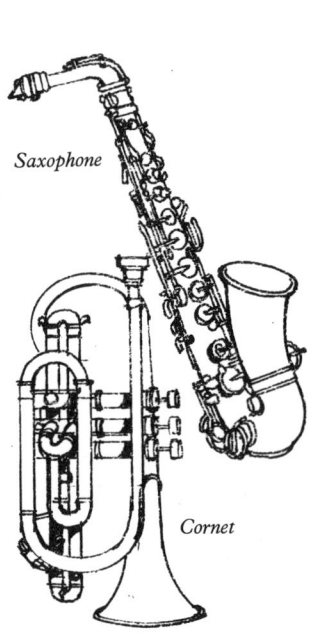

Saxophone

Cornet

Things to do

● Parents and grandparents talk regretfully of the passing of the days when music-making at home was more common. On the other hand, though many tried to sing and most at least started to learn the piano, it did not often get much further than that and the music itself was really no better or worse than a modern popular song or light classic.

Perhaps the main reason for less home music now is lack of *space* rather than inclination. Compact flats and the single living–dining room do not encourage activities like music. Those who do play and sing go out to folk clubs, choirs, amateur orchestras, and attend weekend courses or summer schools rather than confine their music-making to their own homes.

● Interview people in local amateur orchestras, choral societies, operatic societies. Find out what sort of people they are, their jobs, etc., and why they enjoy amateur music. Find out how the societies are organized, how they started, what their problems are. Record some of the music they make.

● Find out what openings there are for amateur musicians within ten miles of your home. Make a list and offer it for display in your public library.

5 · Public Entertainment

(Note: many aspects of this section are dealt with in *Music and Musicians*.)

The only public music available up to the time of Pepys and Purcell was the street ballad-singer, the band of the 'town waits' and any religious or royal procession that might chance to come by. Ballad-mongers plied their trade till the end of Victoria's reign, selling cheaply printed 'broadsides' or chapbooks containing the words of old ballads and topical songs to be sung to some well-known tune. They were augmented in Victorian times by street musicians–Italian organ grinders and German bands, black-faced minstrels and Irish harpers. In fact the streets of London were a battle ground of competing beggar-musicians and there was a continual stream of complaints in the press about the row that people had to endure throughout the day.

The first public concert open to anyone for the price of a ticket was put on in December 1672, following this announcement in the press:

... to give notice that at Mr John Banister's House (now called The Music School) over against The George Tavern in Whitefriars, near the back of the Temple, this Monday, will be music performed by excellent masters, beginning at precisely 4 of the clock and evry afternoon for the future, precisely at the same hour.

right: *Italian street musician playing a hurdy-gurdy with dancing dolls c. 1875.*

far right: *Organ-grinders at the turn of the century.*

THE TRUMPET SOUNDS
A
VICTORY.

◆◇◆◇◆

HE was Fam'd for Deeds of Arms,
   She a maid of envy'd charms,
Now to Him her love imparts,
  One pure Flame pervades both hearts:
Honour calls him to the Field,
   Love to conquest now must yield,
Sweet maid he cries, again I'll come to thee!
  When the glad Trumpet sounds a Victory.

Battle now with fury glows,
   Hostile blood in torrents flows,
Hit duty tells him to depart,
  She press'd her Hero to her heart!
And now the Trumpet sounds to Arms,
  Amidst the clash of rude alarms,
       Sweet maid he cries, &c.

He with love and conquest burns,
   Both subdue his mind by turns,
Death the Soldier now enthrals,
  With his wounds the Hero falls!
She disdaining war's alarms,
  Rush'd and caught Him in her arms,
O death he cries, thou'rt welcome now to me,
  For hark, the Trumpet sounds a Victory.
       Sweet maid he cries, &c.

Prin

Daniel Wrighton, Printer, Birmingham.

Press complaint ©

It may be admitted that wandering street-players might have been needed formerly; but the whole thing is entirely changed now. Music is to be heard everywhere, by all classes, in their hours of recreation, at proper places and at all prices, from the Italian Opera House to the threepenny gallery at the East-end theatres. There is excellent music, both vocal and instrumental, at such places as the Canterbury Hall, the Oxford, &c. Then take all the choirs in full practice. Look at the monster amateur concerts at the Crystal Palace. It was but the other day advertised that a three-part song for female voices would be done by one thousand voices to each part. Until lately, a very nice little orchestra could be heard by taking a penny ice in Hungerford Market. Think of the thousands of charity children who learn to sing. Look at their annual gathering in St. Paul's, and on one occasion in the Crystal Palace, heard by the Queen. Before closing this note, I will send you a list of all the vocal societies now in operation. In short, music is going on everywhere, and at times when people want it and seek it. It is therefore entirely out of place and time when people are busy and do not seek it, and it comes when they neither expect nor require it. I say again, it is for your opponents to state *exactly* when and for whom it is required.

Music in the street during the day is only good for the encouragement of laziness in idle servants; distracting others who live by their brains, and wasting the time of men working outside and inside of houses, as bricklayers, &c., &c. I know it for a fact, as the experience of twenty years in a lodging-house, that a female servant good for anything was always ready and willing to send away an organ-grinder, in spite of the abuse he would heap upon her.

Organs should be done away with at once. They stand entirely alone from among street instruments. Any vagabond who can carry one can play it— that is, grind it by turning the handle, and therefore can continue the annoyance longer than any other street musician, without having been at the pains and trouble of acquiring a certain degree of musical skill. The sound of an organ is so loud and penetrating, that it is impossible to find a room in an ordinary house where you can escape from it. Organs are especially injurious to the advancement and practice of young learners of the pianoforte, for they not only interrupt their lessons and studies, but actually play off, without the slightest trouble, a tune which has taken perhaps weeks to get through with difficulty, which is very disheartening to the young player. Look at the number of music-teachers who are annoyed in giving their lessons by street musicians. Why should a man, who has spent years in acquiring skill in his profession, who pays high rent and heavy taxes, be robbed of his time, while a vagabond, who pays neither one nor the other, grinds two or three streets out of as many pence?

left: *A broadside*

right: *A modern one-man band*

below: '*The supper at Vauxhall*' by *G. Cruikshank*.

By the end of the seventeenth century London had many music rooms advertising concerts by distinguished Italian and German musicians and the fashion continued at full strength through the whole of the next century. J. C. Bach, Mozart, Haydn and Corelli all appeared frequently at The Stationers' Hall, York Buildings, Hickford's Rooms, Hanover Square Rooms, Covent Garden, Drury Lane, The King's Theatre and the Haymarket. Dublin, Newcastle, Edinburgh and Bristol all had their concert rooms too.

There were also the 'pleasure gardens'—what we would call public parks. But they had bandstands and offered concerts of songs and light music every evening. The main London ones were Vauxhall and Ranelagh (in the Chelsea Embankment area) and musicians like Arne, C. F. Abel and J. C. Bach were at different times responsible for the music. They continued to be popular well into the 1800s but were eventually drowned out and built over with the coming of railways and dense housing. Their place was taken by the Crystal Palace concerts and later by the 'promenade concerts' started at Drury Lane by a colourful French conductor–showman, Louis Jullien. They were called 'promenade concerts' because people were invited to stroll around, chat and take refreshment during the music. The programmes were amazingly varied—from half a Beethoven symphony to a patriotic ballad to a solo on the musical saw. When the 'Proms' were taken to the Queen's Hall and then to the Albert Hall they became rather more strictly symphonic but still refreshingly informal and friendly.

Some well-known 'pleasure garden' songs

'I Attempt from Love's Sickness to Fly'	H. Purcell
'The Lass with the Delicate Air'	M. Haydn
'Cherry Ripe'	C. Horn
'The Ploughboy'	W. Shield
'The Lass of Richmond Hill'	Anon.
'Lo, Hear the Gentle Lark'	H. Bishop
'Now Phoebus Sinketh in the West'	T. Arne
'Sally in our Alley'	H. Carey
'Tom Bowling'	C. Dibdin

The lighter music then moved into the public parks again—and the seaside bandstands and hotel lounges where little

right: Jullien's Concert Orchestra with military bands at Covent Garden Theatre.

below right: Sir Charles Groves conducting the BBC Symphony Orchestra at the last night of the 'Proms', 1974.

orchestras and military bands played selections from musical comedy, Strauss waltzes and concert overtures by Suppé, Hérold, Auber and others. Radio and records and the expense of hiring musicians gradually forced these groups out of existence and we now have very little live music in public places, which seems a pity.

Some of the hotel bands became very popular in the thirties and were the first groups to become famous through radio and recording. These were the dance bands like those of Lew Stone, Ambrose, Henry Hall, etc. They also toured the country appearing in variety theatres, playing current popular songs interspersed with comedy routines.

right: *The Columbians*
far right: *Henry Hall*

right: *Carol Gibbons and the Savoy Hotel Orpheans.*
far right: *Lew Stone and his band.*

right: *Jack Payne and his band.*
far right: *Roy Fox and his band.*

Musical theatre

The most complicated form of musical theatre is opera, which is traditionally rather a prestige form of entertainment often attended by people because they wish to show they can afford it rather than because they really enjoy it. It has always been something of a status symbol, associated with the better-off sections of society. It is very expensive to stage, requiring not only a cast of singers, a chorus and elaborate costumes and sets but also a full symphony orchestra in the pit—and all these people have to be paid. In the seventeenth century when opera began, it was put on mainly at court or in opera houses financed largely by the nobility. Opera houses were more than places of entertainment—they were meeting-places and even eating-places; noble families had their private box with a room behind and used it to entertain guests. Often they paid very little attention to what was going on on the stage. The Paris Opera of the early 1800s was the meeting-place of high society too and a hotbed of scandal and gossip.

As music, opera cannot be lumped all in one heading. There are many different styles and they do not all involve huge sopranos and very high singing. It is easy to make fun of the ridiculous aspects of opera but singing every line of a play is really no more unrealistic than reciting them in verse, as in Shakespeare, or bursting into a song and dance routine on top of an Alp as in *The Sound of Music*. Many operas are quite light and even funny and there are always beautiful tunes to be heard. Some of our most well-known tunes come from opera—Handel's 'Largo', 'The Toreador's Song', 'The Anvil Chorus', 'The Nun's Chorus', 'One Fine Day', 'The Ride of the Valkyrie', etc.

Some of the easiest operas to enjoy:

The Barber of Seville	Rossini
Don Giovanni	Mozart
Der Freischütz	Weber
Carmen	Bizet
The Tales of Hoffmann	Offenbach
Noye's Fludde	Britten
The Rake's Progress	Stravinsky

A scene from Carmen *at the Royal Opera House, London.*

Musical shows

Shows with some music and some speech go under various names—operetta, light opera, musical comedy, musical. One of the earliest in this style was a little French play with music called *Robin and Marion* which first appeared around 1300. Some of Shakespeare's plays have a great deal of music in them—*Twelfth Night*, especially—which almost makes them into musicals. Henry Purcell, in Restoration days, wrote several musical plays and the great French dramatist Molière collaborated with musicians in shows called 'comédies–ballets'—*L'Amour Médecin* and *Le Bourgeois Gentilhomme* were two of them.

This kind of entertainment was much more popular in England than opera—the English never took to opera as well as the Italians and French. *The Beggar's Opera* of 1723 set the pattern for a series of popular entertainments called 'ballad-operas' which continued until the mid-nineteenth century. Later ones were not as good—they were thrown together very quickly and used any old music that was around, rearranged to

suit the occasion. The plots–taken from old fairy tales, the folky setting with squires and woodcutters–and the use of popular songs of the day show where our Christmas pantomime originated. France had these too, called 'vaudevilles' with the same romantic stories and popular tunes used over and over again.

In the mid-nineteenth century, a better-constructed type of light musical show began to appear–the operettas of Gilbert and Sullivan in England–the *opéras-bouffes* of Offenbach in France. Similar shows by Strauss in Vienna (*Die Fledermaus, The Gipsy Baron*, etc.) were followed slightly later by *The*

Merry Widow by Franz Lehár. The Viennese style of operetta even travelled to America in the works of Sigmund Romberg (*The Student Prince, The Desert Song*) and Rudolf Friml (*The Firefly, The Vagabond King, Rose Marie*).

In England, after Gilbert and Sullivan came the musical comedies of the Gaiety Theatre–modern fairy tales about handsome diplomats or millionaires falling in love with shop-girls and struggling actresses (*The Belle of New York, Floradora, The Shop Girl*) these also continued well into the twentieth century in the shows of Noël Coward (*Bitter Sweet*), Ivor Novello (*Glamorous Night*) and Jerome Kern (*Roberta*).

left: *Scene from* The Merry Widow *at Daly's theatre, 1907*.
above: '*Offenbach surrounded by his compositions*' *by A. Gill*.

55

In 1927, Jerome Kern wrote the first truly American musical (*Show Boat*) and from then on, America led the world in light musical theatre with the talents of Gershwin, Porter, Berlin, Rodgers, Loewe, Bernstein and Sondheim.

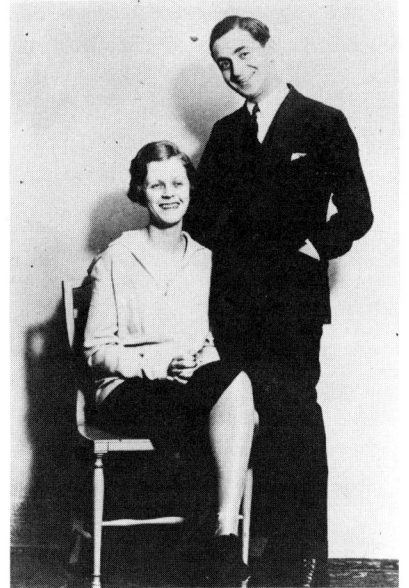

above left: *Irving Berlin and his wife*
above right: *Cole Porter*
right: *George Gershwin*

Music hall

Throughout the second half of the nineteenth century, the 'halls' were the favourite haunt of working-class families, young city clerks and shop-girls, and the songs sung there were the big hits of the day. In the later part of the century, larger, commercial theatres opened giving what was called 'variety'. The audience was now in rows of seats instead of drinking at long tables, the décor was as plush as an opera house and the items were indicated not by a stentorian chairman but by numbers at the side of the stage. The old

A night at the Victorian music hall.

*The Ethiopian
Serenaders*

*A working men's club in
the north of England*

music-hall stars continued to appear in these theatres and the last of them have disappeared only recently. Variety continued longer in France–The Olympia in Paris is still a variety theatre.

Music hall is revived in England at the Players' Theatre under Charing Cross Station and on television. (See also *Music and Musicians*.)

58

SOME OF THE GREAT SONGS OF MUSIC HALL AND VARIETY

'Sam Hall' (W. G. Ross)–c. 1850
'Vilikins and his Dinah'–c. 1840
'Lily of Laguna'–1898
'Waiting at the Church' (Vesta Victoria)–1906
'It's a Great Big Shame' (Gus Elen)
'Knocked 'em in the Old Kent Road' (Albert Chevalier)
'Any Old Iron' (Harry Champion)
'The Biggest Aspidistra in the World' (Gracie Fields)

FROM THE MINSTREL SHOWS

'The Camptown Races'
'The Old Folks at Home'
'I Dream of Jeannie'
'Come where my Love Lies Dreaming'

above: *Harry Champion;* below left: *Gus Elen*
below centre: *Little Tich;* below right: *George Robey*

The Boy in the Gallery by George Ware

A Marie Lloyd number and one of the best of all music-hall songs

I'm a young girl_ and I've just_ come ov-er_ Ov-er from the coun-try where they do things big. And a-mongst the boys I've_ got a lo-ver_ And since I've got a lo-ver, why I don't care a fig. The boy I love is up in the gal-le-ry The boy I love is look-ing now at me There he is, can't you see, wa-ving his hand-ker-chief as mer-ry as a ro-bin that sits on a tree.

Marie Lloyd

Dancing

A whole area of music is closely connected with dancing—music for dancing itself and music based on fashionable dances of the day. In the seventeenth century, the society dances were the Playford dances mentioned on page 37 that are still used in primary schools sometimes—Hunt the Squirrel, Black Nag, Goddesses, etc. They are also still danced by interested adults with great enthusiasm. Some of the figures are very complicated and most satisfying to master. Playford dancing has been called 'the chamber music of the dance'.

In the eighteenth century simpler line dances called 'contra-dances' were popular, also the minuet, the cotillion and the polonaise. In the nineteenth century these continued but were augmented by quadrilles (square dances, virtually) and the famous Viennese waltz and polka. Later it was the turn of the lancers (also a variant of the quadrille) and, in Edwardian times, the tango from Argentina and the slow waltz.

Public dances originally only took place in the lowest bars and taverns but, with the gradual loosening up of society etiquette, 'tea-dances' were introduced in the early twentieth century to which ladies could go unescorted (they could always say they were only there for the tea!). This was the age

right: *A tea-dance*

right: *The tango*
far right: *The cha cha*

of new dance crazes every week and the beginning of the popularity of jazz and jazz-influenced dance bands. In the thirties and forties 'ballroom dancing' was the most popular style but already young people were 'jiving' to the music of the big bands and, after the war, this kind of individual dancing with hardly any reference to a partner became the rule.

The Hole in the Wall (a Playford dance tune)

Things to do

● Take a cassette recorder and see if you can record some music from the street or a club or public house.

● Find out where there is a real street singer or old country singer and record an interview and a song.

● Investigate the history of the local concert halls and theatres. Find out when the last variety theatre closed down and see if anyone can tell you about the shows they used to see there.

● Read:

Lost Empires	J. B. Priestley
Sweet Saturday Night	Colin MacInnes
Working the Halls	Peter Honri
The Good Companions	J. B. Priestley
Songs of the British Music Hall	Peter Davison

● Collect the names and photos and music of all the dance crazes of the last fifty years.

● Complete the calendar of musical shows on page 56 up to the present day.

6 · America

There is no doubt that America has been by far the most powerful influence on music in the twentieth century, just as Germany was in the nineteenth and Italy in the seventeenth and eighteenth.

The first American music (apart from that of the Indians, that is) was taken by the Pilgrim Fathers in the form of English and Dutch Puritan hymns and sacred songs—often sacred words set to old folk-melodies.

The earliest immigrants to America after the English and Dutch pilgrims were further English, Dutch and Germans and later Scandinavians and Irish.

Influences from the folk music of all these countries is to be found in early American music, though the language in all but a very few instances is English.

Many English folksongs travelled to America with early settlers and survived there unchanged for two or three hundred years. Longer in fact than they did in their home country. England became heavily industrialized and urbanized, while great areas of America remained remote and unaffected by civilization right into the twentieth century. The English folksong collector Cecil Sharp was amazed to find hundreds of folksongs and some folk-dances long forgotten in England still being sung in the mountain areas of Eastern America—in Kentucky, the Carolinas and Virginia

The first Sabbath of the Pilgrim Fathers in New England

particularly. Here is one of those songs. You will find the rest in Sharp's big collection *English Folk Songs from the Southern Appalachians*.

In Not-ta-mun town___ not a soul would look up___ Not a soul would look up___ Not a soul would look down___ Not a soul would look up___ Not a soul would look down___ to tell me the way___ to Not-ta-mun town___

2   I rode a big horse that was called a grey mare
Grey mane and tail, grey stripes down his back
Grey mane and tail, grey stripes down his back
There weren't a hair on him but what was called black.

3   She stood so still, she threw me to the dirt
She tore my hide and bruised my shirt;
From stirrup to stirrup I mounted again
And on my ten toes I rode over the plain.

4   Met the King and the Queen and a company of men
A-walking behind and a-riding before
A stark naked drummer came walking along
With his hands in his bosom a-beating his drum.

5   Sat down on a hot and cold frozen stone
Ten thousand stood round me yet I was alone
Took my heart in my hand to keep my head warm
Ten thousand got drowned that never were born.

(See page 39 about 'devil's question' songs'.)

Country music

The recreational music of the American pioneers was usually dance music and tunes of European origin gaining a new accent (as the English language gained a new accent) from the mixture of peoples and traditions now joined together.

The dances were often based on European country-dance patterns, particularly the French quadrilles for four couples (what the Americans called 'square dances') and Irish reels (usually danced in two lines, the sexes facing one another). They also amused themselves with 'play party' songs and games–rather in the German and Scandinavian style–grown-up versions of the old children's singing games and more acceptable in the rather puritan communities than actual dances.

The music for these dances took much from Irish and English folk-dance music but gave it a new colour mainly by the addition of the Negro banjo (quickly abandoned by the Negroes themselves when it was used in minstrel shows) and the guitar to the normal fiddle, pipe or concertina. (See especially *American Folk Tales and Songs* by Richard Chase.)

In the early years of this century, the American country-dance band with its rapid banjo picking and thumping bass rhythm–sometimes with Negro-type improvised instruments like washboard and jug–was used to accompany popular songs of the day–sentimental and semi-religious songs like those sung in English Victorian drawing rooms. Also in the repertoire would be some of the real American ballads and folksongs (not imported from Europe) like 'John Henry' and 'Jesse James'. The special sound of the band, the long-necked banjo, the rather nasal tone of the singers (a Spanish influence?), the very regular rhythm and phrase-length of the songs and the sweet sentimentality of the lyrics produced what we now call American 'country music'. Now it is an enormous trade centred on Nashville, Tennessee and producing records which are a huge success with enthusiasts the world over. It is one of the few examples of a traditional musical style that has grown naturally through the years, and never lost its contact with ordinary people.

Among the celebrated singers who have used this style or been closely influenced by it are Hank Williams, Johnny Cash, Elvis Presley, Roger Miller, Tom Jones and John Denver.

Here is a song from one of the most popular groups of the heyday of country music in America—the twenties and thirties—the Carter Family.

Bury Me Beneath the Willow

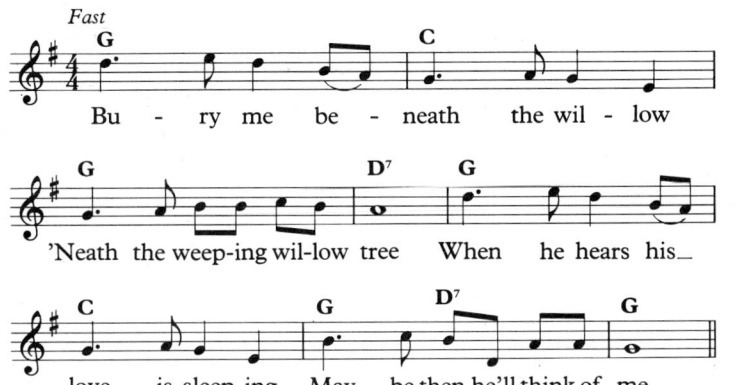

Bu - ry me be - neath the wil - low
'Neath the weep-ing wil-low tree When he hears his_
love is sleep-ing May - be then he'll think of me

Johnny Cash

Elvis Presley   *Roger Miller*   *Tom Jones*   *Hank Williams*

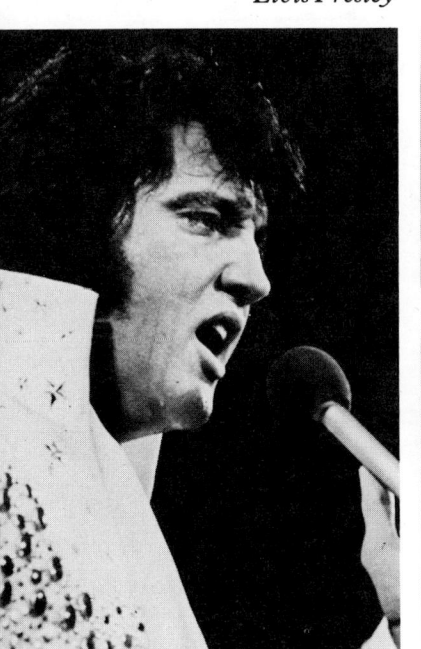

Another group of folk musicians tried to keep to the simpler, more unsophisticated approach, to sing and write songs in country style, not for big money but because they wanted to. The greatest of these was Woody Guthrie who travelled America more or less as a tramp and casual labourer at the time of the big Dust Bowl emigrations so vividly described in Steinbeck's *The Grapes of Wrath*. He wrote and sang songs in folk style to entertain and encourage the poor migrant workers and, often, to attack the greed of those who exploited them.

He was the father of the whole social protest folk-song movement which was carried on by later singers like Pete Seeger, Joan Baez, Tom Paxton, Malvina Reynolds, Woody Guthrie's son Arlo and Bob Dylan.

Union Maid (a Woody Guthrie song to a square dance tune 'Redbird')

There once was a un - ion maid She
went to the un - ion hall When
nev - er was a - fraid Of goons and ginks and
a meet-ing it was called And when the comp'-ny
com-pa-ny finks and the de-pu-ty sher-riffs that
boys_ came round She_
made the raid She al-ways stood her ground O you
can't scare me I'm stick-in' to the Un - ion
I'm stick-in' to the Un - ion I'm stick-in' to the
Un - ion _ O you can't scare me I'm stick-in' to the
Un - ion I'm stick-in' to the Un - ion _
_ till the day I die. _

clockwise: *Woodie Guthrie; Pete Seeger; Joan Baez*

Chicken on the Fence Post (American dance tune)

below: *Bob Dylan;* bottom: *Tom Paxton.*

American Negro music

The Negroes who were brought to America from West Africa were by no means completely primitive in their music. Their West African traditions were quite highly developed especially in the realm of work-songs and ritual dances where their innate sense of rhythm and improvisation were of great importance. This sense of rhythm—not a driving frantic rhythm, but a firm, easy, relaxed beat—coupled with the gift for improvising in singing and playing and, above all, a compulsive, instinctive urge to sing and play at every possible excuse, were the particular musical gifts the African Negroes brought to America and subsequently passed on to the rest of the world.

There are hundreds of books about all the various types of American Negro music of which perhaps the best single work is Harold Courlander's *Negro Folk Music USA* (Columbia UP). We will therefore limit ourselves to listing the main types and leave you to follow them up as you wish.

FIELD HOLLERS

Workers in the fields, slaves or convicts would shout across to each other some simple phrase just to keep in touch or perhaps to ask for news – 'Where you bin?', 'How's your sick wife?', 'How long till sunset?' and to the water boy 'Bring the water over here'.

WORK-SONGS

Work-songs are not as common as is sometimes made out. Shanties are the only English work-songs and it is apparently a particularly African idea to use rhythmic chants to help in some heavy or dull job like tree-felling, hoeing, rowing, hauling timber or cargo, etc. Also African is the typical leader–chorus structure of these songs. A leader sings out a phrase and the rest of the gang reply with a standard chorus or repeat of the leader's phrase.

No More, My Lord (Negro work-song)

BLUES

This is another example of the African Negro's compulsive urge to sing. In this case he sings to himself when he is feeling depressed because, by singing his feelings, he feels he can lighten his worries. Instant psycho-analysis.

There are many fine recordings of very lowly people, often convicts or street beggars, singing completely unaccompanied blues which they make up as they go along. Many of these turned professional in the twenties and thirties and used guitar, harmonica and piano for accompaniment. They sang mainly to their own Negro audiences but in more recent times blues singing has become very popular with students and the blues style has been adapted to electric instruments by Alexis Korner, John Mayall, The Rolling Stones, etc.

Blues with piano was often speeded up and given an insistent, eight quavers in a bar, rolling bass beat over which the singer sang or improvised at the top of the piano. This was called 'boogie' or 'rhythm and blues' and eventually contributed to 'rock 'n' roll' in the late 50s.

There are many fine records of blues in many styles but the standard album (and book) is *The Story of the Blues* by Paul Oliver.

RELIGIOUS MUSIC

Everybody knows some of the famous Negro spirituals like 'Were you there?', 'Swing low sweet chariot', etc. These have in fact strong Western influences from the Methodist hymns the Negroes were taught by white preachers and in the harmonies copied from English hymn harmonization. Perhaps this is why English people like them!

More African and genuinely Negro in manner is the more frantic rhythmic and hypnotic congregational singing of the revivalist Negro services where the preacher (in true African call-and-response pattern) yells out the phrases of his sermon and the congregation shouts back standard phrases like 'Hallelujah', 'Praise the Lord', 'That's right man', 'I know, I know', etc. Then, almost before you realize it, the whole process has become an actual song with verses and chorus, and the drums, harmonium and mouth organ join in as a backing to a new song never heard before and probably never to be sung again. This is a glimpse of the most fascinating processes of primitive, communal music-making clearly owing its origins to similar processes still used in West Africa.

Many of the songs are made permanent of course. We call them 'gospel songs'—and again, as with country music and blues, the style has been brought into commercial pop with great success. All the great Negro singers—Mahalia Jackson, Odetta, Aretha Franklin, Ray Charles, The Staple Singers— use this gospel style. They use it for non-religious music too, when they call it 'soul'. The famous Motown groups—The Supremes, The Four Tops, The Pips, The Vandellas, etc.— base their arrangements on that same leader-and-chorus pattern, with the soloist, like the preacher, singing out the verse and the rest interjecting short repeated chorus phrases.

Aretha Franklin

The Staple Singers

Ray Charles

The Four Tops

The Supremes

JAZZ

Most Negro styles are based on improvised singing and rhythm. Jazz is what happened when this improvised singing and rhythm was put on instruments—the instruments of the military band or brass band (the easiest instruments to make a loud happy noise on—and the cheapest). The early jazz bands were marching bands, very much like our own brass bands and Salvation Army bands. But the Negroes were never satisfied with just playing the tunes and harmonies exactly as they were written down. They wanted to play around with the music as they did with their own tunes. So the brass band marches began to sound very different when the Negroes played them. The instrumentalists gradually got more and more confident on their instruments and started to play not so much for marching but more for dancing.

The rest of the story is well known: the addition of piano, banjo, saxophone, etc., the movement into the white territories of Chicago and New York, the spread of the whole jazz craze in the twenties, the big bands of the thirties and forties and the eventual return of jazz to a specialist popularity with the greater success of rhythm and blues, country music and rock 'n' roll. Some of the old big bands are still around—Duke Ellington, Count Basie, Stan Kenton and some new ones occasionally appear. Old small jazz bands still play too—Eddie Condon, Chris Barber—but rather for minority interests now, though all this music is well worth hearing. Anyway, even if jazz has taken a back seat for the moment, Negro styles still predominate in our popular music today.

King Oliver's Creole
Jazz Band

right: *Stan Kenton*
far right: *Duke Ellington*

right: *Count Basie*
far right: *Eddie Condon*

right: *Miles Davis*
far right: *Chris Barber*

 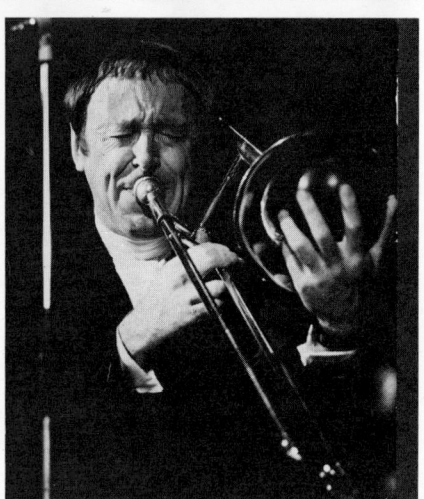

Epilogue

To everything that has been said here about music's place in various societies must now be added the fundamental alteration that has taken place in the whole subject in the last century—the invention of recording and radio. It is difficult for us to imagine what a different thing music was to people without radio and records and how much more 'special' a thing it must have been when it was always 'live' and always an event.

Whether we like it or not, music is now far less of a special event than it used to be—it is as available as water from the tap and, like the ticking of a clock, people hardly notice it till it stops.

Furthermore, it is becoming international—we can hear the music of every country and race and they can hear ours. The latter seems to be more often the case. Far more tragic than the taking for granted of music in the background all the time is the overpowering of the truly national music of countries in Africa and the East by the Western musical 'plastic'.

There are many pros and many cons in this debate and it is encouraging to see that the worst effects of tapwater music have not in fact taken over as completely as was once feared. Perhaps men do unconsciously resist the spiritually as well as the physically harmful.